The Piddle Valley Cookbook

The Piddle Valley Cookbook

The favourite recipes of the people of The Piddle Valley

BARRIE & JENKINS
communica-europa

First published in this edition in 1978 by Barrie and Jenkins Ltd
24 Highbury Crescent London N5 1RX

ISBN 0 214 20505 3

Typeset by Spectrum Typesetting, London N1.
Printed by T. J. Press & bound at
Robert Hartnoll of Bodmin, Cornwall.

Contents

ᐸᗕ Preface ᗧᐳ

When I announced to my congregation in Portsmouth that I
had been appointed to the four churches of the Piddle Valley
in the beautiful and fascinating county of Dorset, the impact was
impressive. Some thought it was just a bad joke; others thought
perhaps I needed a break. But in spite of the general opinion that
the whole thing sounded a trifle unseemly and ought to be
forgotten, my family and I left the city and descended on the
lovely Piddle Valley just in time to celebrate Christmas 1974.

My installation took place in the ancient church of All
Saints, Piddletrenthide, and during the ceremony I couldn't
help but notice the sorry state of the fabric. In 1976 we launched
the Restoration Fund, aimed at raising an initial £10,000
which would allow most of the vital work to be carried out.
The really worrying single item is the growing instability of the
early 15th-century chancel arch. Unless this is corrected the
movement will continue until collapse occurs. The cost of
restoration falls on a small community of some 500 people and
ways and means of raising this 'impossible' sum have been
pursued with enormous enthusiasm. One life-line was thrown
by the Piddle Valley cooks. A small gathering of people banded
together and sent out a call, echoing up and down the valley,
for recipes. The good people of the parishes of the valley —
Piddletrenthide, Piddlehinton, Alton Pancras, Plush and
beyond — responded as only dedicated cooks can and, in the
spring of 1977, their small booklet, *Piddle Valley Cook Book,* was
born. Sales were immediate and contributed handsomely to the
fund. After only six months of fast selling, with copies going all
over the world, our little booklet was 'discovered' by Barrie
and Jenkins. So the original act of faith has been well rewarded.

All Saints Church, Piddletrenthide, dates from the 12th
century and stands in a dominating position on high ground to
the north of the village. Its tower, constructed in 1487, is
considered to be one of the finest in the country and is richly

decorated with splendid gargoyles — one of which is playing the bagpipes!

One of the changing aspects of country life is the gradual disappearance of the old village families. Probably not a great many remain in the valley, but we are fortunate that the 'old' and the 'new' seem to blend well together. Perhaps the new arrivals bring an extra 'something' to the community; certainly the old families offer a sense of continuity and permanency that is so lacking in this age of rapid change.

The Church has long been closely associated with places of refreshment — inns, in other words! In centuries past Christian pilgrims used to find food and shelter in these friendly hostelries as they journeyed on their way. So it's all the more pleasing to me, as Vicar, to know that the inns of the valley (of which there are many) have been happy to be associated with the cook book project by contributing recipes.

Finally, I would like to thank all those who have helped to produce this book — the Piddle Cooks, both named and anonymous. By purchasing this book you will help to preserve Piddletrenthide's beautiful and ancient church for future generations.

Derek Parry
Vicar, All Saints Church, Piddletrenthide

Ode to School Mash

At school we have mash,
which tastes just like Flash,
But we're told it is good for our tummies.
We don't doubt their word,
But the mash is absurd,
And we'd rather have something more yummie.

By Nancy, Ella and Belinda Clark and Colette Coverdale,
Piddletrenthide School

⌒⌐ Piddletrenthide: ⌐⌒
The Village and Its Church

The origins of the village of Piddletrenthide in the Piddle Valley of Dorset reach back into prehistory. Bronze Age man probably lived in the valley — he certainly buried his dead there, as the barrows (burial mounds) still visible in quite a few fields in the parish attest. Iron Age enclosures are also evident, together with traces of the so-called Celtic field systems. The Romans were also present in the valley. Roman roof tiles and the distinctive Samian pottery have been found around Doles Ash Farm in the east of the parish, and a mosaic pavement was apparently found around 1740 in the grounds of the Manor House. Quite likely a Roman villa stood there, as in neighbouring areas, relying on the prosperous town of Durnovaria (Dorchester) for the marketing of its produce.

The first written references to Piddletrenthide are in the Saxon charters. In 891 a charter for neighbouring Plush, now part of the parish, defined the village's northern boundary, and in 966 King Edgar confirmed to the nuns of Shaftesbury Abbey possession of ten 'hides' of land (a 'hide' being merely a method of working out rateable values) at 'Uppidelen', which must refer to Piddletrenthide or its upper tithing. Certainly by Saxon times the village was divided into three tithings: the upper, where the church and Manor House stand; the middle; and the lower, also called White Lackington. Even today, most of the village's buildings are grouped in these three areas.

In William the Conqueror's Domesday survey of 1086 we are told that 'the church of St Peter at Winchester holds Pidrie' It listed three mills along the river Piddle, and part of the village was leased by a knight and a certain widow. The whole village was assessed for thirty hides, a large number. This 'value' also gave the village its present name: literally meaning thirty (using the French word, *trente*) hides on the river Piddle. The word *piddle* means nothing more derogatory than a stream of clear water!

The Abbey of Hyde, formerly St Peter's of Winchester, where King Alfred was buried, remained the owner of the village until the dissolution of the monasteries in the 1530s. The Abbey also maintained a cell or small monastery in the village, which may have lain adjacent to the Manor House. A medieval altar slab which forms part of a fireplace in one of the village houses possibly came from this chapel, which had disappeared by 1382.

By the sixteenth century the village was a thriving community, growing right along the valley bottom. Its nucleus, however, remained the area around the church; a network of lanes, now mostly unused, still radiates from here. This important centre of village life, All Saints Parish Church, stands near the northern boundary of the parish. The earliest reference to it comes from a document of about the year 1000 where it is stated that Emma, the wife of Ethelred the Unready and mother of Edward the Confessor, gave Piddletrenthide with its church to Hyde Abbey.

The church we see today, justly described as one of Dorset's finest, does not appear to contain anything earlier than Norman work, and most of the structure is fifteenth century. The most celebrated feature is, without doubt, the very fine west tower. It belongs to a small group of Dorset towers which have become known as the Dorchester Group. The tower has an amazing array of terrifying gargoyles carved into grotesque figures, one of which is playing an instrument remarkably like the bagpipes! Above the west door of the tower is a Latin inscription: *Est pydeltrenth villa in dorsedie comitatu Nascitur in illa quam rexit Vicariatu 1487* (It is in Piddletrenthide, a town in Dorset [where] he was born [and] where he is Vicar, 1487). It seems, then, that the tower was the responsibility of Nicholas Locke, the vicar at the time. But the most remarkable thing about this inscription is that it is probably the earliest use of Arabic numerals on any building in England, Roman numerals being still used almost exclusively even today. It is also unusual to have a feature such as a tower so closely dated.

The north and south walls of the church date from about 1500; the south wall is particularly notable for the life-like lions carved on the buttresses. The other exterior walls are probably of the early fifteenth century. The church is entered through the fifteenth-century south porch. Above the entrance is a sundial bearing the date 1602 and a now illegible inscription. The doorway is of typically ornate Norman design, and is probably twelfth century which makes it one of the earliest parts of the church. Near the south door stands the font with its fourteenth-century stone base, and seventeenth-century oak cover.

An inventory of 1552 mentions five bells in the tower, and this was the number until 1972 when a sixth — a treble cast at the famous Whitechapel foundry — was added. The tenor bell, dated 1631, bears the rhyme: 'Com when I call/To serve God all.' The chancel arch is mostly of the early fifteenth century, but the base on the south side is undoubtedly twelfth century, with the base on the north side cut to match it at a later date. The oak communion table in the south aisle is an unusually fine example of early seventeenth-century woodwork. According to a former vicar, this table was for many years in the bar of one of the village pubs and was brought back to the church to serve its original purpose at the end of the last century.

In 1543, after Henry VIII dissolved Hyde Abbey, the village was granted to Winchester College who remained the principal owners until the 1950s. Quite a few houses in the village have complete lists of their 'copyholders', or tenants, from the sixteenth century until recent days, still held in the archives of the College.

On 2 May 1654, a fire destroyed many houses in the village. Help came quickly for those made homeless, initially from the Corporation of Dorchester who, the next day, ordered that '£5 is to be sent immediately to Pudletrenthead for the supply of necessityes of the poore people whose houses were burnt yesterday'. On 14 May a further £18 19s 2d (a very large sum in those days) was sent to the village, the money having been collected in the streets of Dorchester. Help also came from as far as Hampshire, Somerset and Wiltshire. Perhaps it was after the fire that the village moved away from the lanes around the church and spread along what is now the main road.

The principal family of the Manor House for many years was the Colliers. One of the last members of the family built the existing house towards the end of the eighteenth century. In 1812 the lease was acquired by the Bridge family. They were well known as jewellers and silversmiths, and were responsible for making the Crown of State for Queen Victoria, still worn by the sovereign for the opening of Parliament. The present school building was provided by John Bridge in 1848. The most remarkable feature of this school are the gates. They were once in Westminster Abbey and are popularly supposed to have surrounded the tomb of Mary Queen of Scots, although some experts consider the tomb to have been that of Lady Margaret Beaufort, mother of Henry VII. Bridge acquired the ironwork after its removal from the Abbey after a particularly drastic restoration in 1826.

During the nineteenth century the population grew, from 449 people in 1801 to 680 in 1831. It might have increased further had plans for a canal and even a branch railway been implemented. In 1852-53 the church received a fairly thorough restoration, though much less extreme than some of the work done in other churches in the same period, being concerned primarily with putting to rights the neglect of time, such as rising damp and rotting woodwork. The architect of this restoration was John Hicks who, in 1856, was to take the young Thomas Hardy, born four miles away, as his pupil. Hardy may have visited the church during his time with Hicks for, in the south aisle wall of the churchyard, there are two small rounded tombstones of the Dumberfield family, both dated 1616. The family, although with better-known associations with Bere Regis a few miles away, were immortalised by Hardy in his *Tess of the D'Urbervilles*. Other members of the family are recorded in the parish registers. Also buried in the churchyard are Ralph Wightman, the well-known author and broadcaster, whose family has been in the area for centuries and who himself was born in the village in 1901, and Sir Henry Jackson, the famous general, who died in 1972.

Andrew Pike

Soups

Soups

Watercress Soup

1 bunch of watercress	Salt if needed
$\frac{1}{3}$ level teaspoon (1 ml) freshly grated nutmeg	$1\frac{1}{4}$ (725 ml) milk
	1 chicken stock cube
1 oz (30g) flour	A good shake of onion salt
$1\frac{1}{2}$ oz (40g) butter	Double cream
Black pepper	Paprika

Wash and pick over watercress, removing any yellow leaves and about 2 inches (5 cm) of the lower coarse stalks. Make a roux with the butter and flour and $\frac{1}{4}$ pint (150ml) of the milk. Blend the cress and the pint of milk very thoroughly in liquidiser and add to the roux, mixing well. Crumble and add stock cube, shake in onion salt, nutmeg and black pepper to taste. Test for salt. Bring very slowly to the boil, stirring all the time. Do not allow to boil hard. Serve topped with a swirl of thick cream and a decorative shake of paprika, and with fried bread croûtons on the side.

Mrs M. D. Davidson, Piddlehinton

Courgette Soup
(Serves 8)

3 lb (1.35K) courgettes	Pepper and salt
2 chicken soup cubes	$\frac{1}{2}$ pt (275ml) clear chicken stock
Small knob of garlic	
2 lb (900g) onions	5oz (145g) double cream
1 tablespoon (20ml) sour cream	Oregano

Slice onions and fry in butter with a small knob of garlic, pepper and salt until onions are very well cooked. Slice courgettes and boil until soft, then strain and liquidise. Dissolve soup cubes in one pint of water, add chicken stock and a shake of oregano, and simmer for 5 to 10 minutes. Stir in the double cream and allow to cool. Then put into refrigerator until required. Serve hot or cold, adding spoonful of sour cream at the last moment.
Note: Overgrown courgettes can be used up in this way. If

chicken stock is not available substitute by using 3 cubes in one and a half pints of water. The cream is not essential but some cream, particularly sour cream, adds considerably to the soup's flavour and texture.

Brian Till, Piddletrenthide

Lettuce Soup
(A good way of using up lettuces which have gone to seed)

Any number of lettuces	Milk
2 large onions	Dessertspoon sherry
4 large potatoes	Cornflour for thickening
Chicken stock	Sour cream or yogurt

Chop the onions and saute them in a little butter until soft but not browned. Add the potatoes cut in small pieces and as many shredded lettuces as you like. Cover with milk and chicken stock (half and half) and a dessertspoon of sherry. Stew until the potatoes are cooked and then add seasoning and liquidise in an electric blender. Return to saucepan and thicken with a little cornflour if necessary. Add a swirl of sour cream or yogurt to each serving.

'Defrosting' Soup

When the day dawns to de-frost the freezer, have ready a large saucepan and into it place the last six months' savoury left-overs which have found their way into the freezer (omitting elastic bands, tie-tags and odd bits of suet!). Cover with ½ gallon (2.3l) of stock (also found in the freezer). Add 2 to 3 large onions, 8 oz (225g) split peas, season to taste and cook until tender. Liquidise and return to the freezer until required.

Soups

Apple Soup

3 large cooking apples
2 onions
1 oz (30g) butter
1 oz (30g) cornflour

4 cloves
2 oz (55g) brown sugar
1 qt (1.25l) milk and water
Seasoning

Peel, core and slice apples. Melt butter in a large pan, add apples and fry very gently for 10 minutes. Cut onions in half and stick a clove in each half. Add onions, sugar, seasoning and liquid to pan and simmer gently for an hour. Remove from heat and sieve soup or put in an electric blender (taking care to remove the cloves). Return to pan, bring to boil and thicken with cornflour.

C. Keller, The European, Piddletrenthide

'Cheat' Soup

Tin of tuna fish
Stock
Cream
Sherry or brandy

Tin of condensed asparagus
 soup
Tin of condensed mushroom
 soup

Liquidise tuna, soups and stock. Heat through. Add more stock for right consistency. Season. Add sherry or brandy and cream.

Jillie Edwards, Piddletrenthide

Piddle Potage

1½ lb (680g) beetroot, cooked, skinned and grated
2 oz (55g) butter
1 large onion, finely chopped
2 oz (55g) plain flour
3 pt (1.75l) chicken stock

2 tablespoons (40ml) red wine vinegar
1 teaspoon (4ml) ready-made mustard
3 tablespoons (60ml) cream

Cook the onion in the butter until soft. Add the flour and cook for a further few minutes. Pour on the stock and bring to the boil. Add the grated beetroot and the vinegar and season well. Simmer for about 20 minutes and then liquidise. Return the soup to the pan and stir in the mustard. Adjust the seasoning, add the cream and stir until boiling. Cook for 3 minutes.

Elizabeth Larpent, Piddlehinton

Dot's Curried Vegetable Soup

2 carrots
1 onion
1 potato
1 small can tomato purée

2 pt (1.15l) stock
1 oz (30g) margarine
Salt and pepper
1 teaspoon (4ml) curry powder

Prepare vegetables and put through mincer. Melt margarine in pan, add vegetables, curry powder, purée, and cook slowly for five minutes. Add stock. Bring to the boil and simmer for 30 minutes.

Mr Hilton

Vichyssoise

3 large leeks, well washed
and discarding only a very
little of the green part
2 large potatoes
1 large onion
2 pt (1.15l) chicken stock

1½ oz (45g) butter
Salt and pepper
1 egg yolk
¼ pt (150ml) single cream
Chives

Chop the onion and cook it in the butter for 5 minutes, being careful not to brown it. Add the leaks, sliced thinly, and the potatoes, diced. Cook for a further 3 minutes and then pour on the chicken stock and the seasoning. Simmer for about ½ hour, until the vegetables are cooked. Liquidise or put through a sieve. Add the beaten egg yolk. Chill. Just before serving, add a swirl of cream to each helping and a scattering of snipped chives. True vichyssoise should be served cold, but it is almost as nice served hot, in which case the egg yolk should be omitted.

FROM THE PAST

An Excellent Soup for the Weakly

Put two cow heels and a breast of mutton into a large pan with four ounces of rice, one onion, twenty Jamaican peppercorns and twenty black, a turnip, a carrot and four gallons of water; cover with brown paper and bake six hours. (From *The Modern Cookery* by a Lady, published by J. and C. Mozley, London 1856)

J. E. Morris, Piddletrenthide

Fish

Sea Bass
(old Lincolnshire recipe)

Bass is a game fish and should be hung for 3 to 4 days before
eating. Remove the scales with a sharp knife, clean the fish and
remove head. Make a stuffing with breadcrumbs, mixed herbs to
taste, the grated rind of a lemon and a little juice, a knob of
butter and one egg to bind. If too stiff add a little water. Fill the
cavity with stuffing and sew up. Rub butter over the fish, wrap
in foil and cook in oven at 375°F, Gas Mark 5 (190°C) allowing
15 minutes per pound. Remove foil, lay rashers of bacon over
the fish and place under the grill until the bacon is done, turning
once. Serve with a rich brown gravy and Duchesse potatoes.
This recipe can be used with grey mullet or fresh haddock.

Mrs R. Wright, Piddletrenthide

Trout in Mushroom Sauce
(Serves 4)

4 10-oz (280g) trout	Seasoning
1 pt (575ml) Béchamel sauce	2 oz (55g) butter
12 oz (340g) mushrooms	

Cut the trout lengthways from the top to bottom. Melt the
butter in a frying pan and fry the trout, two halves at a time and
skin side up for about 5 minutes. Then turn the two halves over
and fry for a further 5 minutes. During this time remove the
bones from the flesh, made easier now that the flesh is cooked.
When the skin side has been cooked turn over again and peel off
skin. Repeat with the other trout. During this time fry
mushrooms and add to the Béchamel sauce. Place trout in a dish
and cover with the mushroom sauce. Serve hot.

William Till, Piddletrenthide

Crispy Fish Pie

¾ lb (340g) coley fillet (it will turn white after being cooked)
2 hardboiled eggs
5 oz (145g) flour

3 oz (95g) butter
4 oz (115g) grated Cheddar cheese
Parsley and seasoning

Cover the fish with milk and cook until tender. Pour off the milk. Flake the fish and put it in a shallow dish with the sliced hardboiled egg on top. Make a thick white cheese sauce with the milk, 1 oz (30g) of the butter, 1 oz (30g) of the flour and 2 oz (55g) of the cheese. Add the parsley and seasoning and pour over the fish and egg. Rub the remaining butter into the rest of the flour until it is like fine breadcrumbs. Stir in the remaining cheese and sprinkle the mixture over the fish. Bake in a moderate oven until the top is golden and crisp.

Doris Moore, The Green Dragon, Piddletrenthide

Portland-Style Mackerel

4 fresh mackerel
Salt and pepper
Flour

Sauce

8 oz (225g) gooseberries
2 oz (55g) sugar
2 tablespoons (40ml) water
1 oz (30g) butter
Pinch nutmeg

Clean and split mackerel. Season with salt and pepper and dust with flour. Grill until golden brown. Cook gooseberries with sugar and water until tender. Put through a sieve, add butter and nutmeg. Reheat and simmer for 5 minutes. Serve sauce with mackerel, hot or cold.

John Firrell, Piddletrenthide

F*ish*

Fish Casserole
(Serves 4)

1 lb (455g) fillet of white fish
Salt
Pepper
Lemon juice
1 small onion, sliced very
   thinly

4 tomatoes, peeled and sliced
2 tablespoons (40ml) grated
   cheese
2 tablespoons (40ml)
   breadcrumbs
½ oz (15g) butter

Trim the fish, season with salt and pepper and lemon juice and
arrange on a fire-proof dish. Add onion and tomatoes. Mix
cheese and breadcrumbs together and sprinkle on top. Dot with
butter and bake about 20 minutes in a moderate oven (375°F,
Gas Mark 5 or 190°C).

Joan Ralph, Piddletrenthide

Poor Man's Smoked Salmon

Use one packet of kipper fillets. Lay them in a shallow dish,
sprinkle with lemon juice, pour oil over them and leave for 24
hours, turning once. Eat with brown bread and butter.

Amy Till, Piddletrenthide

Salmon Kedgeree

2 oz (55g) butter
7-8 oz (185–225g) tin
  salmon
Small onion
1 teaspoon (4ml) sugar
3 eggs

1 tablespoon (20ml) sultanas
Good pinch curry powder
3–4 sprigs of parsley
1 cup (180g) rice
Seasoning

Soak the sultanas in hot water. Fry the onion with the sugar.
Hard boil the eggs. Cook the rice. Remove any skin and bone
from the salmon, saving the juice from the tin. Melt the butter
in a pan and add the cooked rice, salmon and juice, chopped
parlsey, sultanas, two of the eggs (chopped), curry powder,
seasoning and more butter if necessary. Transfer to a casserole
and chop the remaining egg for garnish on the top.

Jane Gordon, Piddletrenthide

Salmon Mousse

1 large tin salmon
3–4 tablespoons (60–80ml)
  white sauce
½ pt (275ml) aspic jelly

¼ oz (7g) gelatine
¼ pt (150ml) double cream,
  whipped
1 egg white, whipped

Pound the salmon (having removed any skin and bone) and mix
in the white sauce and some seasoning. Prepare the aspic jelly
and line a mould with a little of it, decorating with green peas,
etc. if required. Put into refrigerator to set. Dissolve gelatine in a
little cold water and add to remainder of hot aspic. Add this to
salmon and also the whipped cream and whipped white of egg.
Pour into the mould. When set turn out and garnish with
cucumber or watercress.

Jane Gordon, Piddletrenthide

Hot Crab and Garlic Pâté
(Serves 6)

½ lb (225g) white crab meat
2 oz (55g) sage and onion
   stuffing mix
½ lb (225g) butter
1 lemon

1 teaspoon (4ml) tomato
   purée
4 large cloves of finely
   chopped garlic

Add enough eoiling water to the stuffing mix to make a thick
paste. Melt the butter in a saucepan and add the garlic and crab.
Simmer for a few minutes. Then add the stuffing, tomato purée
and juice of one lemon. Stir well. To serve, place in an ovenproof
dish (individual ones are best) and place in a very hot oven until
the top starts to get crisp. Garnish with a slice of lemon and
parsley.

The Old Bakehouse, Piddletrenthide

Yummy Tuna Flan

6 oz (170g) puff pastry
8 oz (225g) canned tuna
   (flaked)
2 teaspoons (7ml) grated
   lemon rind
Salt and pepper
2 eggs

¼ pt (150ml) milk
¼ pt (150ml) cream (or top of
   the milk)
2 oz (55g) cooked peas
2 tomatoes, skinned and sliced
Stuffed olives and parsley to
   decorate

Roll out pastry thinly and line an 8-inch (15cm) flan or pie plate.
Bake blind in a hot oven for 10 minutes. Mix tuna, lemon rind
and seasoning to taste. Beat eggs, milk and cream and add to
tuna mixture with peas and tomatoes. Pour into flan case. Bake
at 375°F, Gas Mark 5 (190°C) for ½ hour. Decorate.

Jillie Edwards, Piddletrenthide

Marinated Smoked Herrings

Remove the skin from kipper fillets and build them up in layers in a jar or basin. Between each layer put thinly sliced onions, whole black peppercorns and an occasional bay leaf. Cover with vinaigrette and keep in the refrigerator. They are ready to eat after about three days and keep at least three weeks.

The vinaigrette can be your own favourite recipe. What we use is about 80 per cent oil and 20 per cent vinegar with rosemary, French mustard, sugar and seasoning.

The Old Bakehouse, Piddletrenthide

Fried Herrings

One herring per person. Ask your fishmonger to split and bone them. Sprinkle with lemon juice and dip in medium oatmeal seasoned with salt and pepper. Fry on both sides until a nice nutty brown colour.

Amy Till, Piddletrenthide

Poultry and Game

Mustard Chicken
(An unusual flavour. Serves 4)

4 raw chicken joints
2 oz (55g) butter
2 teaspoons (7ml) Worcester
   sauce
Salt and pepper
1 oz (30g) flour
½ pt (275ml) hot water
¼ pt (150ml) double cream
2 tablespoons (40ml) oil
2 tablespoons (40ml) dry
   mustard
1 chicken stock cube

<u>Garnish</u>

Watercress
Skinned and baked small
   tomatoes
1 oz (30g) flaked almonds
   (browned)

Heat oil and butter, toss chicken joints in seasoned flour, and fry gently on both sides until golden brown and tender. Arrange in shallow baking dish. Dissolve stock cube in the hot water, stir in mustard and Worcester sauce, pour over chicken, cover and bake about one hour or until tender. Just before serving stir in cream, scatter almonds and garnish with cress and tomatoes.

                                        Mrs M. D. Davidson, Piddlehinton

Crunchy Crisp-Baked Chicken
(Serves 4)

2 rounded tablespoons (50ml)
flour

¼ rounded teaspoon (1ml)
curry powder

4 chicken quarters

2 packets of potato crisps (50–60g)

1 rounded teaspoon (5ml) salt

A little creamy milk

Preheat oven to 350°F, Gas Mark 4 (180°C). Mix flour, salt and curry powder. Crush potato crisps with a rolling pin. Coat chicken joints with the seasoned flour. Dip joints into milk and coat thickly and evenly with potato crisp crumbs. Arrange skin side up on a baking sheet. Bake for 40–50 minutes. Serve hot or cold with green salad or fried potatoes.

Jill Uht, Piddletrenthide

Creamy Chicken Curry (Cold)
(Serves 6)

1 chicken

2 oz (55g) mango chutney

2 fluid oz (65ml) dry white
wine

2 oz (55g) honey

¼ pt (150ml) double cream

½ oz (15g) medium curry
powder

10 oz (280g) mayonnaise

Garnish

Flaked browned almonds

Sliced pimento

Cucumber

Put honey and curry powder into a pan and simmer very gently for 10 minutes. Add chutney and wine and cook for a further 5 minutes. Pass through a sieve and cool. Whip cream and fold into mayonnaise. Add prepared curry mix, blending well. Fold in the finely sliced (or diced) flesh of the cold cooked chicken. Pile into a suitable dish, sprinkle with the almonds and garnish with the cucumber and pimento. Serve with very dry, well-separated boiled long grain rice in a separate dish.

Mrs M. D. Davidson, Piddlehinton

Condon's Chicken Concoction

3 lb (1.35K) chicken, cooked and cut up
1 oz (30g) chopped onion
1 tablespoon (20ml) cooking oil
1 teaspoon (4ml) curry powder
1 dessertspoon (10ml) of red jelly jam (any variety)
1 teaspoon (4ml) tomato purée
½ wineglass red wine
½ wineglass water
Salt and pepper
1 teaspoon (4ml) lemon juice
¼ pt (150ml) double cream
2 tablespoons (40ml) mayonnaise
3 oz (95g) raisins

Fry the onion lightly in the oil. Add curry powder and cook for 2 minutes. Stir in the jelly, tomato purée, red wine and water. Bring to the boil. Season and add the lemon juice. Simmer for 10 minutes. Cool. Lightly whisk the cream, fold in the mayonnaise and curry sauce. Mix the chicken with the raisins and toss everything together. Serve cold with a salad, or it is delicious served hot with rice and vegetables.

Audrey Condon, Piddletrenthide

Chicken-in-a-Blanket

1 boiling fowl
3 onions, chopped
½ lb (225g) mushrooms
   (chopped field mushrooms
   are best, but whole button
   mushrooms may be used)
3 oz (95g) butter
3 tablespoons (60ml) flour

½ wineglass dry Vermouth
1 wineglass cheap white wine
Salt and pepper
Bouquet garni
1 egg yolk
Juice of half a lemon
¼ pt (150ml) cream

Put the chicken in a pan with an onion and a carrot, and simmer until tender. Remove from pan, cut into pieces, arrange in a deep dish and keep hot. Fry onions in butter until soft but not brown. Stir in the flour and add enough chicken stock, with a little milk, to make a fairly thick white sauce. Add the mushrooms, the Vermouth and wine, the seasoning and the bouquet garni, and simmer for about 20 minutes. Beat the egg yolk into the lemon juice. When the sauce is ready, take it off the heat, remove the bouquet garni, stir in the egg and lemon mixture and add the cream. Pour the sauce over the chicken. Serve with long-grain rice.

Sweet-and-Sour Chicken and Bacon

4 rashers bacon
12 oz (340g) cooked chopped
   chicken
3 tablespoons (60ml) cooking
   oil
1 chopped onion
2 carrots
1 small hard white cabbage
2 oz (40ml) mushrooms

For the sauce

2 teaspoons (7ml) sugar
1 tablespoon (20ml) vinegar
1 heaped teaspoon (5ml)
   cornflour
2 teaspoons (7ml) soya sauce
¼ pt (150ml) water
1 dessertspoon (10ml) tomato
   ketchup
Salt and pepper

Chop bacon and place in frying pan with oil. Fry for a few minutes, add chicken and heat through. Remove to a plate. Cut carrots into long strips, chop cabbage finely, chop mushrooms, and put all these in the frying pan. Fry gently with the chopped onion for 15 minutes. Make the sauce by mixing the cornflour with the water to make a paste. Add the sugar, tomato ketchup, vinegar and soya sauce. Put the mixture into a frying pan. Add the bacon and chicken, with salt and pepper. Cover with a lid and cook slowly for 15 minutes. Serve with boiled or fried rice as preferred.

Mrs J. Anderson, The Thimble, Piddlehinton

Casseroled Chicken with Wine
(Serves 6)

1 small tender chicken or 6 portions
$\frac{1}{2}$ oz (15g) flour
Salt and pepper
2 tablespoons (40ml) oil
2 small onions, peeled and sliced
2 carrots, peeled and sliced
2 oz (55g) mushrooms, peeled and sliced
$\frac{1}{4}$ pt (150ml) dry white wine
$\frac{1}{2}$ pt (275ml) chicken stock
Bouquet garni
1 tablespoon (20ml) chopped parsley

Joint and skin chicken, coat with seasoned flour and brown all over in heated oil. Remove chicken and fry vegetables. Put vegetables into a casserole, arrange chicken on top and add stock and wine. Tuck bouquet garni in centre. Cover closely and cook in slow oven (350°F, Gas Mark 4 or 180°C) for about $1\frac{1}{2}$ hours. Remove bouquet garni and correct the seasoning. Sprinkle with chopped parsley.

Joan Ralph, Piddletrenthide

Turkey Shepherdess
(A way of using up the remains of the Christmas bird)

In a double saucepan make a custard with ¾ pt (425ml) of milk and 3 egg yolks. Fry ½ lb (225g) of chopped onions in a little butter. Add 1 lb (445g) of chopped cold turkey and ½ lb (225g) of chopped cooked ham. Stir in a dessertspoon (10ml) of tomato purée. Put the meat in an oven dish, pour the custard over it and sprinkle with 3 oz (95g) of grated cheese. Brown in the oven for about 20 minutes.

Using Up Cold Turkey

Cold turkey   6 tablespoons (120ml)
1 tin of tuna fish   mayonnaise
1 small tin of anchovies

Arrange slices of cold turkey on a dish. Put the tuna fish, anchovies and mayonnaise in an electric blender and convert into a smooth sauce. If it is too thick, add salad oil until it is of a good consistency. Pour over the turkey and garnish with tomato and cucumber. Left-over chicken can be used in the same way.

Muriel Pike, Piddletrenthide

Poacher's Pie

First catch (or buy) your rabbits (two small ones are best), skin
them and cut into small joints. Simmer gently and when soft
push into a pie-dish into which 2 sliced hardboiled eggs have
been arranged round the side. Save the liquor in which the rabbit
has been cooked and thicken with $\frac{1}{2}$ oz (15g) powdered gelatine.
Pour this over the rabbit. Over the top place a pastry cover,
decorate with pastry leaves and roses, and bake in a fairly hot
oven. Eat cold.

Peggy Cake, Plush

Venison

Bone a saddle of venison and marinate in red wine with 2 bay
leaves, 1 sliced onion, 2 cloves garlic and 2 tablespoons (20ml)
olive oil. Leave in the marinade for four days turning twice daily.
When removed from the marinade, lay flat and place rashers of
streaky bacon over it, then roll up like a Swiss roll and tie
securely. Make a good gravy to which a glass of red wine is
added. Place venison and gravy in a casserole and cook in a slow
oven (350°F, Gas Mark 4 or 180°C) until the meat is tender.
Serve with mashed potatoes, swedes and carrots.

Mrs R. Wright, Piddletrenthide

Meat

PORK

Hubble Bubble

1 lb (455g) potatoes, cooked and sliced	4 rashers streaky bacon, de-rinded and chopped
8 oz (225g) skinless pork sausages, halved	1 medium onion, peeled and chopped
2 eggs	$\frac{1}{4}$ pt (150ml) milk

Prepare vegetables and bacon. Place potato slices in a pie dish. Fry bacon without any extra fat, until the fat from the bacon melts. Add chopped onion and the sausages. Fry for 5 minutes, remove from frying pan and drain on kitchen paper, then place on top of potatoes. Beat the eggs with the milk, add salt and pepper and pour into the pie dish. Bake in oven until custard is set, 30 minutes at 375°F, Gas Mark 5 (200°C). Delicious served with spinach.

7-Layer Dinner

Place in casserole:
1-inch (2cm) layer raw potatoes sliced
Layer sliced onion
1-inch (2cm) layer sliced carrots
Sprinkle $\frac{1}{4}$ cup (45g) rice
Tin of peas with liquid, plus salt and pepper to taste
Layer of pork sausages or pork chops (if latter, trim fat)
Pour tin of tomato soup diluted with water over top.
Bake in moderate oven for about 2 hours.
Cover casserole for first hour only.
A very tasty supper dish.

Jenny Sherwood, Piddletrenthide

M*eat*

Sausagemeat and Bramleys
(Serves 4)

1½ lb (680g) sausagemeat
1 hardboiled egg (chopped)
1 egg (beaten)
2 Bramley apples
1 tablespoon (20ml) parsley
   (chopped)

3 tablespoons (60ml) dried
   breadcrumbs
1 medium onion (chopped)
Salt and pepper
2 tablespoons (40ml) melted
   butter

Roll out the sausagemeat (this is easier if you chill the meat first
and use a well-floured board). Peel, core and finely dice the
apples. Mix with the chopped onion and hardboiled egg, stir
in the parsley, salt and pepper. Spread this mixture on to the
sausagemeat, roll up and place on a baking sheet. Turn the
breadcrumbs in hot butter until all are coated, brush the
sausagemeat loaf with beaten egg, scatter breadcrumbs over the
surface and bake at 350°F, Gas Mark 4 (180°C), for 45 minutes.

Hopel-Popel

1 lb (455g) boiled potatoes
   (diced)
1 medium onion (peeled and
   finely chopped)
4 large eggs

4 oz (115g) button mushrooms
   (sliced)
2 oz (55g) grated cheese
4 oz (115g) streaky bacon
   (de-rinded and diced)

Prepare potatoes, mushrooms and bacon. Fry the bacon, onions
and mushrooms gently, then add the potatoes and allow to
warm through. Beat the eggs, pour over the potato mixture,
sprinkle with grated cheese and cook slowly until the eggs are
set. Brown the top under the grill, cut into wedges and serve
piping hot.

Friday Pie
(Serves 4)

Pastry Case

Sift 8 oz (225g) plain flour with a pinch of salt. Add 4 oz
(115g) butter. Rub fat into flour and add 2 tablespoons (40ml)
cold water. Mix together, adding another tablespoon of water
if too dry. Roll out the pastry and line a 6-inch (12cm) to
7-inch (14cm) sandwich tin.

Filling

4 rashers of bacon	3 oz (90g) Cheddar cheese
1 egg	(grated)
Pepper	2 tomatoes (skinned and
1 tablespoon (20ml) milk	chopped)

Trim the rind off the bacon and cut into small pieces. Then
put half this amount into the pastry case, followed by half the
amount of grated cheese. Put half the chopped tomatoes on top
of the cheese. Repeat with bacon, cheese and tomato. Break the
egg on top of this mixture. Roll out the remainder of the pastry
and put over the top of the pie. Cut three slits in the top and
brush with milk. Bake near top of oven at 400°F, Gas Mark 6
(200°C), for 25 minutes until top is golden brown.

Fiona Geffers, Piddletrenthide

M*eat*

Pork Chops In Cider

4 pork chops (lean if possible)
½ pt (225g) still cider (¼ pt
   or 115g stock and ¼ pt or
   115g cider may be used if
   preferred)

1 medium-sized onion
1 tablespoon (20ml) flour
2 oz (60g) butter
1 teaspoon (4ml) Bovril

Brown the pork chops in butter in a frying pan and then lay
them in a casserole dish. Slice the onion thinly and cook in the
frying pan till lightly brown. Arrange the onions on top of the
pork chops. Make a roux with the flour and butter in the frying
pan. Then add the cider gradually to make a smooth sauce.
Add a teaspoon (4ml) of Bovril and seasoning, stirring well.
Pour the sauce over the pork chops. Cover the casserole with a
lid and put in a moderate oven at 375°F, Gas Mark 5 (190°C)
for ¾ to 1 hour.

Johanna Geffers, Piddletrenthide

Sauté Liver
(Delicious quick liver dish. Serves 2)

¼ lb (115g) liver
2 cloves garlic
1 teaspoonful (4ml) chopped
   parsley

Oil
Salt and pepper
Lemon juice
Handful of breadcrumbs

Cut liver into thin strips. Rub in salt and pepper. Cook in oil
until brown all over. Add chopped garlic and parsley. Cook
slowly for about 5 minutes. Add breadcrumbs and fry for
further 2 minutes. Add juice of a lemon. Serve with rice or
vegetables.

Ian Condon, Dorchester

Saucisses au Vin Blanc

Sausages
Butter
Sprinkling of flour
2 tablespoons (40ml) cream
Slices of bread fried in butter

Glass of white wine (I have used cider as an alternative and it is excellent)
Salt and pepper

Put sausages in pan with plenty of butter and place in moderate oven. When half cooked sprinkle with a little flour, add wine, season with salt and pepper and simmer on slow fire until done. Just before serving, mix in the cream. Have the slices of bread ready, fried to a golden brown in butter. Put on a hot dish and lay the sausages on them. Pour the sauce over them and serve very hot.

Noel Slade, Plush

Bacon Roly-Poly

Suet crust

8 oz (225g) self-rising flour
4 oz (115g) suet
$\frac{1}{4}$ pt (150ml) water

Filling

$\frac{1}{2}$ lb (225g) collar bacon
Onion, chopped
Apple, sliced
Sage

Make suet crust and roll out to an oblong shape $\frac{1}{4}$-inch ($\frac{1}{2}$cm) thick. Lay bacon over pastry and sprinkle with sage, chopped onion and sliced apple. Dampen edges and roll up as Swiss roll. Wrap in greased grease-proof paper and foil. Steam for $2\frac{1}{2}$ hours.

M*eat*

Pork Chops with Anchovies
(Serves 6)

6 pork chops
3 oz (95g) butter
2 eggs, lightly beaten
Dried breadcrumbs
Seasoned flour

Anchovy butter
8 anchovy fillets
3 oz (95g) butter
2–3 sprigs parsley
Freshly ground pepper

Dip pork chops first in flour, then in egg and lastly in the breadcrumbs which should be well pressed in. Melt the fat in the pan, and fry the chops on each side until the coating is a rich brown. Place them with any remaining fat from the pan in an oven-proof dish with a lid. Put in the oven (350°F, Gas Mark 4 or 180°C) for 35 minutes. Pound the anchovies and blend them with the butter, pepper and chopped parsley. A knob of anchovy butter should be placed on each chop just before serving.

Jane Gordon, Piddletrenthide

Pork with Prunes

2 fillets of pork
1 dozen large prunes soaked
  overnight in $\frac{1}{2}$ pt (275ml)
  cider
Seasoned flour

2 oz (55g) butter
$\frac{1}{4}$ pt (150ml) double cream
1 dessertspoon (10ml)
  redcurrant jelly
Salt and pepper

Place soaked prunes and cider in a saucepan and simmer for 30 minutes. Cut pork fillet into 1-inch (2cm) pieces and bang flat. Coat the pork in seasoned flour and fry gently in butter on both sides until cooked through (about 15 to 20 minutes). Transfer to casserole dish. Drain the prunes, reserving the liquid, and arrange round the pork. Add the prune liquor to the juices in the pan and stir in the cream and redcurrant jelly. Heat through until the jelly is dissolved. Season with salt and pepper, pour over the pork and prunes and continue to heat in a slow oven until required.

Jane Gordon, Piddletrenthide

Leeks and Bacon
(Serves 3 to 4)

An extraordinarily good dish that hails from Lorraine where it is called 'Poireaux à la paysanne'. Particularly economical if you can get hold of some bacon scraps.

Dice 4 oz (115g) of bacon and fry in butter in a stewpan. Peel, wash and cut a bundle of white leeks (about 1½ lb or 680g) into pieces about an inch long. When the bacon is well fried and lightly browned add the pieces of leek and cook them gently for half an hour, stirring them frequently. When they are done, salt them lightly and serve very hot.

A. H. Waterfield, White Lackington

Liver and Bacon Pâté

12 oz (340g) ox liver	¼ pt (150ml) milk
1 oz (30g) cornflour	1 egg
Salt and pepper	1 oz (30g) butter
6 oz (170g) bacon pieces	Sprinkling of mixed herbs

Make thick white sauce with butter, cornflour and milk. Mince liver and bacon, and blend with the sauce. Add beaten egg and season. Pour into greased loaf tin, cover with greaseproof paper. Bake 1 hour at 375°F, Gas Mark 5 (190°C). Turn out when slightly cool. Freezes well.

Sally Condon, Dorchester

M*eat*

Sweet-and-Sour Sausages
(A change from the usual weekday dishes. Serves 4)

½ green pepper
2 rings canned pineapple
1 medium-sized onion
½ oz (15g) margarine
2 rounded teaspoons (4ml)
  cornflour
2 tablespoons (40ml) pineapple
  syrup
1 level tablespoon (20ml)
  chutney

3 level teaspoons (12ml)
  tomato purée
2 teaspoons (7ml) soy sauce
2 level teaspoons (7ml) caster
  sugar
1 tablespoon (20ml) vinegar
½ pt (275ml) water
1 lb (455g) pork sausages
  (skinless are very nice)
8 oz (225g) long grain rice

Slice green pepper into strips, remove seeds and core and white pith. Place in a small saucepan, cover with water and cook for 3 minutes. Drain. Cut pineapple into pieces. Peel and slice onion. Melt margarine in a medium-sized saucepan, add onion, cook without browning for about 3 minutes. Stir in cornflour, pineapple syrup, chutney, purée, soy sauce, sugar, vinegar and water. Bring to the boil, stirring. Fry sausages until golden brown, cut into pieces, add to sauce and simmer for 10 minutes. Add pineapple and green pepper, bring back to the boil, simmer for 5 minutes. Cook rice in a large saucepan in boiling salted water. Drain. Arrange rice on a warmed serving dish and pour sweet and sour sauce on top.

Patricia Weeks, Piddlctrenthide

Middle Tything Brawn

½ pig's head or 1 lb (455g)
  belly pork
Pig's trotter

1 calf's tongue
¾ lb (340g) shin of beef

Soak the pig's head overnight. Boil all meat together until it falls from the bone. Skin tongue. Chop and mix together all meats, place in oblong lunch box, cover with strained liquor and leave to set.

Piddle Pork

1½ lb (570g) pork (fillet, loin or belly)
Onion
Flour
½ pt (275ml) stock

Sherry
Tomato purée
Salt and pepper
6 oz (170g) mushrooms

Cut the pork into 1½-inch (3cm) pieces and fry gently. Put into casserole. Fry onion lightly, add flour and cook one minute. Remove from heat and add stock, a little sherry, tomato purée, salt and pepper. Return to heat and simmer to thicken. Pour over meat and place in oven for 1 hour at 350°F, Gas Mark 4 (180°C). Add 6 oz (170g) mushrooms five minutes before serving and stir in cream to taste.

M^{eat}

Apricot-Stuffed Tenderloin of Pork
(Serves 4)

2 tenderloins of pork
(approx. 1 lb or 445g each
in weight)
1 cup (180g) white breadcrumbs
1 chicken bouillion cube
$\frac{1}{4}$ lb (115g) dried apricots
or 1lb (455g) fresh apricots
(if using dried apricots
these should be put to soak
in water the previous
evening)

1 medium sized onion,
finely chopped
2 dessertspoons (20ml)
freshly chopped parsley
Salt and pepper
3 oz (95g) butter
1 teaspoon (4ml) powdered
sage
1 beaten egg
1 small glass dry white wine

Trim the tenderloins so that they are almost identical in shape. Season with salt and pepper and allow to stand while you make the stuffing. Saute the onion in half the butter until tender but not brown. Turn into a mixing bowl with the melted butter from the pan. Add the sage, breadcrumbs and parsley. Put aside eight of the nicest-looking apricots and roughly chop the remainder. Add chopped apricots to the stuffing and bind with the beaten egg. You may need a little stock to mix the stuffing thoroughly. Season with salt and pepper. Flatten the fillets as much as possible with a rolling pin by giving them a few sharp whacks. Spread the stuffing on one and lay the other on top, folding the tapering ends in order to keep a good shape. Tie the fillets with white string or strong double thread, an inch apart. Place in a roasting tin, spread the remaining butter on top and put into a pre-heated oven at 355°F, Gas 4 (180°C). Cook for $1\frac{1}{4}$–$1\frac{1}{2}$ hours, basting with some of the wine and the juices from the pan frequently. Half an hour before the pork is ready, place the remaining apricots in the pan and baste these also. To serve, cut the string and lay the fillets on a heated serving dish and arrange the apricots along the top. Add a little more wine to the juices in the pan, bring to boil on top of stove, scraping up all the brown bits, season if necessary and serve separately. Carve the stuffed meat into one-inch (2cm) thick slices.

Mrs C. R. Williams, Piddletrenthide

BEEF

Hunter's Stew

1 lb (455g) minced beef (raw or cooked)	2 large onions, sliced
	2 large cooking apples, sliced
1½ lb (680g) cooked potatoes, sliced	½ pt (275ml) stock

Arrange alternate layers of potato, onion and apple in a casserole, ending with potato. Season the stock and pour it over the meat. Sprinkle with breadcrumbs and a little grated cheese, and bake in a moderate oven for about an hour.

Flintcombe Veal
(Serves 4)

4 escalopes veal, 4/5 oz (25g) each	1 small chopped fried onion
	Mixture of coconut and breadcrumbs for coating
4 oz (115 g) chopped cucumber	

Mix and season cucumber and onion. Spread evenly over beaten escalopes, and then fold escalopes in half. Dip in beaten egg and then in the crumb mixture. Fry gently in butter on both sides until cooked and golden brown, about 3 minutes each side. Serve with cucumber and yogurt dressing (finely chopped cucumber in natural yogurt).

G. Jakeman, Piddletrenthide

M*eat*

Veal in Wine

2 lb (900g) breast of veal (cut
in 2-inch or 4cm squares)
1½ tablespoons (30ml) flour
Bouquet garni
1 tablespoon (20ml) tomato
purée

1 tablespoon (20ml) olive oil
1 cup (180g) white wine
Salt and pepper
4 sliced onions
2 oz (55g) butter
1 cup (180g) stock

Melt butter, add oil and brown the veal in it. Add onions, salt
and pepper and cook gently for another 5 minutes. Sprinkle on
the flour and mix well. Add the wine, slowly stirring all the
time, and then the stock followed by tomato purée and the
bouquet garni. Continue stirring until sauce thickens. Cover
saucepan and simmer gently until veal is tender (1½ to 2 hours).

Frankie Potter, Piddletrenthide

Beef Goulash

1½ lb (680g) skirt of beef
(in 1-inch or 2cm cubes)
1 clove garlic (crushed)
1 tablespoon (20ml) flour
Salt and black pepper
2 oz (55g) butter
1 dessertspoon (10ml) paprika
pepper

1 pt (575ml) stock (from beef
cube)
4 oz (115g) fresh soured cream
2 onions (sliced)
¼ teaspoon (1ml) cayenne
pepper
2 tablespoons (40ml) tomato
purée

Brown meat in butter. Remove and put in casserole. Fry onion,
garlic, paprika, cayenne and flour for 1 minute in dripping or
butter. Add stock, purée and seasoning and stir well. Pour over
meat, cover and cook (300°F, Gas Mark 4 or 150°C) in the
lower half of an oven for 2 hours. Add soured cream
immediately before serving.

Hilda Matthews, Piddletrenthide

Savoury Mince Cobbler

1 medium onion
1 small packet frozen mixed
   vegetables
1¼ lb (570g) minced beef
1 oz (30g) margarine
¾ pt (425ml) water
1 beef cube
1½ oz (45g) flour
Seasoning

For topping
6 oz (170g) self-raising flour
1 level teaspoon (4ml) salt
1½ oz (45g) margarine
¼ pt (150ml) milk

Set oven at 425°F, Gas Mark 7 (220°C). Peel and roughly chop onion. Melt margarine in pan, add onion and fry for 4 to 5 minutes. Add minced beef and quickly fry for a further 2 to 3 minutes. Stir in flour and beef cube dissolved in water. Bring to boil. Add mixed vegetables and seasoning and mix well. Turn into a shallow 1½ to 2 pint (850ml to 1.15l) ovenproof dish. *Topping:* Sift flour and salt. Rub in margarine until mixture resembles fine breadcrumbs. Stir in milk and mix to a soft dough. Turn on to a floured board and knead lightly until smooth. Roll out to ¾-inch (2cm) thickness and cut into 2-inch (4cm) rounds. Arrange on top of casserole and brush with a little milk. Bake for about 20 minutes until golden brown and well risen.

Mrs Jamieson, Piddletrenthide

Meat Loaf
(Serves 6)

1 lb (445g) lean stewing steak   4 oz (115g) fresh white
2 eggs   breadcrumbs
½ lb (225g) streaky bacon   Black pepper and grated
1½ cloves garlic, crushed   nutmeg to season

Mince meat and bacon together – fairly finely. Add
breadcrumbs, garlic and half teaspoon nutmeg, and season with
pepper to taste. Bind with the two eggs (well-beaten). Press the
mixture into a buttered basin, allowing room for rising, cover
with foil and steam for 2½ hours. When cold turn out, brush
with melted butter and roll in fresh or toasted breadcrumbs.

Mrs M. D. Davidson, Piddlehinton

Stewed Calves Tongue

Well wash tongue in salted water. Put in saucepan with one or
two onions, carrots and bay leaf, and salt to taste. Simmer 1½ to
2 hours. Remove from saucepan and peel off the coating from
the tongue. Keep hot while thickening the liquid with flour or
cornflour – serve this with the tongue. A delicious and
nourishing meal.

Mrs I. R. Aldridge, Alton Pancras

Abbot's Ford Tongue

1 salted ox tongue (with all the gristly bits cut away)

For the sauce

2 large onions, chopped	A little flour
2 tablespoons (40ml) of cheap red wine or sherry	2 tablespoons (40ml) tomato purée
$\frac{1}{4}$ lb (115g) mushrooms, sliced	Stock or gravy

Simmer the tongue until tender in water containing 1 onion stuck with cloves and 1 carrot. (I prefer to boil the tongue until, when prodded with a fork, it is as soft as butter – about 3 to 4 hours depending on size.) Take out of the water and skin. Then place in a large basin, cover with a plate or saucer and press with weights on top. Leave overnight. For the sauce, saute chopped onions until soft. Add enough flour and stock to make a thick sauce. Add mushrooms, tomato purée and wine. Turn the tongue out of the basin and slice on to a deep dish (leaving enough to have cold the next day as it is so nice!). Pour the sauce over it, and place in a low oven until ready to serve.

Muriel Pike, Piddletrenthide

M*eat*

Enchilladas with Ratatouille
(This sounds very exotic but is really only a super way of using up cold meat)

I cannot give quantities because they depend entirely on the number of pancakes required.

For the Pancakes
Flour, eggs, milk, pinch of
    salt, butter for frying

For the Filling
Minced cold beef (or lamb)
Onions, two cloves of garlic,
    tomato purée, gravy or
    stock
A little oil for frying

For the Ratatouille
Onions and tomatoes, plus mushrooms, aubergines, courgettes and green peppers as available.

Make as many pancakes as required, as paper-thin as possible. Put on one side. Put a little oil in a saucepan. Fry chopped onions until soft. Add minced meat, two cloves of garlic chopped small or put through a garlic press, tomato purée (about two tablespoonsful), and a little gravy or stock until the mixture is squishy but not too wet. If liked. liven up with a hint of Worcestershire or soy sauce. Put a tablespoonful of filling on each pancake and roll up. When all the pancakes are filled, sprinkle them with Parmesan cheese, put side by side in a deep dish, cover with foil and put in a low oven to warm through.

For the ratatouille, put a little oil in a frying pan. Slice onions and fry until soft. Add sliced courgettes (unpeeled), sliced tomatoes (peeled by spearing each with a fork, holding it for a moment in boiling water, withdrawing it and removing skin), green peppers (cored and de-seeded), sliced mushrooms and aubergines. Cook until vegetables are soft but not soggy. Drain from oil.

Remove foil from pancakes, put ratatouille round them and serve.

Muriel Pike, Piddletrenthide

LAMB

Kiddles Kidneys

12 lamb's kidneys
2 oz (55g) butter
1 oz (30g) flour
1 onion, chopped

$\frac{1}{2}$ pt (275ml) stock
6 tablespoons (120ml) dry
   wine or sherry

Melt butter and lightly fry the onion and halved kidneys until they are brown and firm (about 2 minutes). Remove pan from heat, blend in flour, stock and wine or sherry, season and bring to boil. Cover pan and simmer for 10 minutes until kidneys are cooked. Pour into a dish and sprinkle with parsley.

Aunt Julia's Lamb En Croûte

1 large boned and rolled
   shoulder of lamb
$\frac{1}{2}$ lb (225g) flaky pastry

Stuffing

1 onion
$\frac{1}{4}$ lb (115g) mushrooms
2 tablespoons (20ml) chopped
   parsley
Salt and pepper
Garlic
Butter

Chop onions and mushrooms *very* finely. Crush garlic. Fry in butter with parsley until soft. Stuff this into the pocket of the lamb where the bone was. Roll and string and roast at 350°F, Gas Mark 4 (180°C) for $1\frac{1}{2}$ hours. Leave to cool. Make gravy in normal way, adding a dash of brandy. Trim fat off outside of joint. Make pastry and roll into oblong, wider than the length of the joint and 4 times the width. Then cut into one-third and two-thirds. Wrap the two-thirds round the joint, leaving a gap at the top. Roll remaining one-third out a little longer and put over top. Seal and brush with egg. Decorate and cook for about 40 minutes.

Jillie Edwards, Piddletrenthide

M*eat*

Baked Lamb Chops with Tomatoes and Cheese

4 lamb chops
1 oz (30g) fat
2 large onions
$\frac{3}{4}$ lb (340g) canned tomatoes
$\frac{1}{2}$ level teaspoon (2ml) salt

$\frac{1}{4}$ level teaspoon (1ml) pepper
1 level teaspoon (4ml) sugar
2 oz (55g) grated cheese
2 oz (55g) fresh breadcrumbs

Trim excess fat and remove bones from the chops. Peel and slice the onions. Grate the cheese and prepare the breadcrumbs. Brown the chops in the hot fat and place in a large shallow casserole in a single layer. Lay the onions on top of each chop. Pour on the tomatoes, add seasoning and sugar. Mix the cheese and breadcrumbs and spread them thickly over the chops. Cover and bake slowly, for $1\frac{1}{2}$ hours at 325°F, Gas Mark 3 (170°C).

Gina House, White Lackington

Purbeck Meat Balls

1 breast of lamb
1 egg
1 tablespoon (20ml)
   breadcrumbs
$\frac{1}{2}$ level teaspoon (2ml) salt
Pepper
$\frac{1}{2}$ level teaspoon (2ml) nutmeg
$\frac{3}{4}$ teacup (125ml) milk

1 beef cube
1 chopped onion
2 tomatoes
4 tablespoons (80ml) melted
   margarine
1 level tablespoon (20ml) flour
$\frac{3}{4}$ pt (425ml) boiling water
2 lb (900g) mashed potatoes

Simmer breast of lamb in stock for $1\frac{1}{2}$ hours. Remove meat and mince. Mix meat with beaten egg, breadcrumbs, seasoning and nutmeg. Bind together with milk. Form into small balls. Lightly fry chopped onion in oil or margarine. Remove to casserole with chopped tomatoes. Brown meat balls and place in casserole. To remainder of margarine in frying pan, add flour and cook for one minute. To this add beef cube dissolved in the $\frac{3}{4}$ pint (425ml) of boiling water. Cook for one minute and pour over meat balls in casserole. Arrange mashed potatoes around meat and bake in moderate oven for 30 minutes.

John Firrell, Piddletrenthide

Admiral Hardy's Old English Lamb

1 leg of lamb	Pepper and salt
½ oz (15g) cooking fat	1 large orange
¾ oz (20g) plain flour	2 tablespoons (40ml) clear
¾ pt (425ml) vegetable stock	honey
Sprigs of mint	2½ lb (1.15K) potatoes

Pre-heat oven to 350°F, Gas Mark 4 (180°C). Peel potatoes and parboil for 5 minutes. Melt cooking fat in roasting tin and add parboiled potatoes. Scrub the orange and grate rind. Place rind, honey and ½ level teaspoon (2ml) salt in a basin and mix together. Remove pith from orange with a sharp knife and cut across in 6 slices. Score fat of meat in a diamond pattern. Put in roasting tin with the potatoes and spread with orange and honey glaze. Cook in centre of oven for 2 hours, basting meat and potatoes occasionally. Lift lamb and potatoes on to warm serving dish and keep hot. Strain most of the fat from the roasting tin, stir in the flour and vegetable stock and bring to boil. Taste and season and pour into warm gravy boat. Arrange slices of orange, slightly overlapping, with sprigs of mint along meat. Arrange potatoes around meat. Serve with green vegetables.

John Firrell, Piddletrenthide

Neck of Lamb with Butter Beans

Depending on the number for which the dish is to serve, soak butter beans overnight in water.

Next day drain off water and place beans at the bottom of a casserole. Cover with a layer of sliced onions and on top place the joints of neck of lamb. Add stock made of Oxo cube or Marmite and water to cover beans and onions, and season. Cover casserole and bake in slow oven 225°F, Gas Mark $\frac{1}{4}$ (110°C) or in bottom of a Raeburn for 6 to 8 hours.

Mr Taylor, Wimborne

Traditional Toad-in-the-Hole

2 or 3 sheep's kidneys	6 oz (170g) flour
Sliced cold mutton (or other cold meat)	1 pt (575ml) milk
	2 eggs
A few mushrooms (optional)	Salt and pepper

Stew kidneys in a little stock until tender. Place meat, kidneys and mushrooms (if used) in a buttered ovenproof dish. Make a batter with the flour, eggs, milk and seasoning. Pour over meat. Bake in hot oven until batter is well risen and golden.

C. Keller, The European, Piddletrenthide

Vegetable and Salad Dishes

Herb Pudding
(Oven method)

Gather any greens available – Easter magiants (bistort), nettles, dandelion leaves, a few blackcurrant leaves, onion, leek, a bit of cabbage or curly kale. Wash and dry in a cloth, chop up finely and place in a pie dish with a handful of oatmeal and one of barley. Salt and pepper to taste. Cover with water and leave overnight for oatmeat and barley to swell. Cook same amount of time as cooking a roasting joint, about 1½ hours or more. Stir occasionally to keep from sticking to the dish. If dish is greased first, it doesn't stick so much. Just before serving, add a beaten egg and place in the oven for a few more minutes.

Mrs D. Coulthard, Piddletrenthide

Anne's Cucumber Mould
(This recipe comes from New Zealand)

½ pt (275ml) minced cucumber
¼ pt (150ml) whipped cream
½ packet of powdered gelatine
  (to make 1 pt, 575ml)

1 teaspoon onion juice
Pepper and salt
2 teaspoons (7ml) white wine
  vinegar

Dissolve gelatine *very thoroughly* in a little water, add the vinegar and onion juice to it. Mix well into the cucumber and cream, set into mould and refrigerate for several hours. Can be used as a dish on its own in a cold buffet or salad meal, or can be set in a ring mould and the centre filled with diced chicken and peppers, or shrimps, or flaked salmon lightly turned in mayonnaise, as a light lunch dish.

Mrs M. D. Davidson, Piddlehinton

Leek Flan
(Serves 4)

8 oz (225g) short crust pastry
1 oz (30g) flour
4 oz (115g) strong grated Cheddar cheese
1 lb (455g) leeks

½ pt (275ml) milk
1 oz (30g) butter
1 level teaspoon (4ml) made mustard

Line a flan tin or fluted flan ring with pastry. Bake 'blind' for 15 minutes in a moderately hot oven, remove paper (and whatever you usually use for blind cooking), and return to the oven for a further 10 minutes. Cut leeks across in ¼-inch (½cm) rings and wash well. Melt ½ oz (15g) butter, add leeks, cover and cook over moderate heat for approximately 10 minutes. Melt remaining butter, stir in flour over gentle heat until absorbed. Add milk and cook until sauce is smooth and thick. Season to taste and stir in mustard and grated cheese. As soon as cheese has melted stir in leeks. Pour mixture into warm flan case and serve at once.

Mrs C. R. Williams, Piddletrenthide

Parsnips Au Gratin
(This is a dish which goes well with ham, bacon or
sausages and can take the place of potatoes)
(Serves 6)

2 lb (900g) parsnips
2 tablespoons (40ml) single
   cream or top of milk
2 oz (55g) grated Cheddar
   cheese
Juice of ½ lemon

Salt, pepper and a pinch of
   nutmeg
2 tablespoons (40ml) fresh
   white breadcrumbs
2 oz (55g) butter
½ teaspoon (2ml) dry mustard

Peel parsnips, chop them roughly and boil in salted water to
which the lemon juice has been added, until tender. Drain well
and mash until smooth with a potato masher. Mix in the
mustard, add half the butter and milk or cream and beat well
until the mixture is really smooth. Season with salt, pepper and a
pinch of nutmeg. Spread parsnips in a lightly greased baking dish
or Pyrex plate. Top with the breadcrumbs mixed with the cheese
and dot with the remaining butter. Bake for about 20 minutes in
hot oven (400°F, Gas Mark 6 or 200°C) until hot through and
golden brown.

Noel Slade, Plush

Green Nettle Bake

Choose fresh young nettle tops (and don't sting yourself while
picking them!). Boil 1½ lb (680g) of the tops for about 10
minutes. Squeeze out the water and chop them as you would
spinach. Beat 2 eggs in 5 oz (145g) of sour cream and stir in ¼ lb
(115g) grated Cheddar cheese. Add the chopped nettles. Season
with salt, pepper and a sprinkling of nutmeg. Put in a greased
loaf tin and stand this tin in another one with water halfway up
the side. Cover with foil and bake for about an hour in a
moderate oven.

A Green Dish
(Serves 4)

My parents never called it anything more. It has proved popular on many occasions with the family and friends.

2 eggs
3 tablespoons (60ml) grated Parmesan cheese (Cheddar can also be used)
1 teacup (150ml) milk
½ lb (225g) spinach
½ lb (225g) carrots
2 teaspoons (7ml) minced onion
1 lb (445g) potatoes
Salt and pepper
Mustard

Boil the vegetables, strain and allow to cool. Mince fine and mix with onion, half of the cheese, salt, pepper and mustard, the milk and the egg yolks, well beaten. When this is all well mixed, add the beaten egg whites. Put it into a buttered mould, sprinkle the rest of the cheese and some breadcrumbs over it. Put into a hot oven for 15–20 minutes until surface is brown.

A. H. Waterfield, White Lackington

Sunset Ring
(A spectacular dish for a luncheon party)

$\frac{3}{4}$-pt (425ml) tin of tomato juice

1 teaspoon (4ml) tomato purée

$\frac{1}{2}$ oz (15g) gelatine

1 teaspoon (4ml) sugar

Lemon juice and a strip of lemon rind

Peppercorns, bay leaf, salt, pepper, clove of garlic

Put the tomato juice, tomato purée, sugar and lemon rind in a pan with a few peppercorns, a bay leaf, salt and pepper and a crushed clove of garlic. Bring slowly to the boil and simmer for 5 minutes. Strain and make up with water to $\frac{3}{4}$ pint (425ml). Stir in the gelatine softened in 3 tablespoons (60ml) of warm water and add the lemon juice to taste. Cool, pour into a wetted ring mould and refrigerate. Unmould by standing for a moment in hot water. Fill the centre with shredded lettuce and chopped hardboiled eggs.

Stuffed Tomatoes

8 large tomatoes

3 rashers of bacon, grilled and chopped

3 oz (95g) grated hard cheese

2 onions, sliced and fried

4 oz (115g) white breadcrumbs

Salt, black pepper, oregano, parsley

2 oz (55g) butter

Cut 'lids' off top of the 8 tomatoes, carefully remove pulp from inside and stand 'cases' in ovenproof dish. Melt butter in large pan until frothy, add breadcrumbs, chopped bacon, fried onion, tomato pulp, generous pinch of oregano, salt and fresh black pepper (dried parsley can also be added). Mix well together and then fill tomato cases with 'stuffing'. Bake in hot preheated oven for 20 minutes. Serve with chops, gammon, cutlets, etc.

Sallie Firrell, Piddletrenthide

Orange-Flavoured Potato
(Excellent to serve with game, poultry or gammon)
(Serves 6)

To six servings of boiled potatoes, which should be very
creamily mashed with a good lump of butter, add the grated rind
of a good sized orange, and the strained juice – possibly a little
more than half of it. Blend very well together and serve as you
would an ordinary dish of mashed potatoes.

Mrs M. D. Davidson, Piddlehinton

Rumble Thumps

1 lb (455g) mashed potatoes	1 lb (455g) cabbage, shredded
2 oz (55) butter, cut into	and boiled
pieces	1 large onion, chopped and
4 oz (115g) grated cheese	boiled

Mix together potatoes, cabbage, onion, butter, salt and pepper.
Place in a greased ovenproof dish and cover with cheese. Heat
thoroughly in oven (20 minutes at 400°F, Gas Mark 6 or 200°C)
until the cheese is browned on top. Serve with sausages, if liked.

Crunchy Potato Logs

1 lb (455g) potatoes, mashed	Chopped salted peanuts
and seasoned	1 egg, beaten

Shape the potato into logs $2\frac{1}{2}$ inches by 1 inch (6cm by 2cm).
Dip in egg and then in peanuts and deep fry until crisp and
golden. Decorate with a sprig of parsley.

Honey Roast Potatoes

1 lb (455g) potatoes, peeled	2 tablespoons (40ml) sage and
1 tablespoon (20ml) honey	onion stuffing
1 large onion, sliced into rings	2 oz (55g) butter

Place potatoes in a roasting tin and sprinkle with stuffing and onion rings. Pour over the honey and dot liberally with butter. Bake in oven (400°F, Gas Mark 6, 200°C) for 1 hour or until golden.

Russian Cabbage

Shred 1 red cabbage and cook in about ½ pint (275ml) vinegar rapidly and then drain. When cooked, sprinkle with:

1 peeled and chopped apple	A pinch of pepper, spice and
1 dessertspoon (10ml) vinegar	cinnamon
or lemon juice	A knob of butter
A little sugar	A small amount of fried onion

Reheat cabbage and garnish with triangles of toast. Very good if made with red wine instead of vinegar.

Mrs Dickinson, Wyke Regis

Cauliflower Fritters

Wash cauliflower and break into sprigs. Cook in boiling salted water until tender. Drain. Make up a thick, coating batter and add to it some grated cheese. Dip each sprig of cauliflower into the cheese batter and deep fry until golden. Dry well on kitchen paper. A little grated cheese may be sprinkled over the finished dish.

C. Keller, The European, Piddletrenthide

Blackberry, Apple and Ham Salad

2 Golden Delicious apples
4 oz (115g) lean ham
3 oz (95g) cottage cheese
1 pinch chives

1 teaspoon (4ml) English
  mustard
4 oz (115g) blackberries

Dice the apples and ham. Thoroughly mix the cheese with the chives and mustard in a large bowl. Mix in the diced apples, ham and blackberries and serve on a bed of chopped lettuce and garnish with watercress.

Joan Chandler, Brace of Pheasants, Plush

Hawaiian Sunset Salad

1 cup (180g) grated carrot
½ cup (90g) finely chopped
  salted peanuts

4 tablespoons (80ml) salad
  cream
4 pineapple rings

Mix together carrot, peanuts and salad cream. Place pineapple rings on a bed of lettuce and top each with a spoonful of carrot mixture.

Chinese Salad

Cook ½ lb (225g) long grain rice and rinse under the cold tap. Put in a salad bowl and pour in sufficient salad oil to coat and glisten the grains. Add the contents of a tin of sweet corn, two sticks of celery (chopped), ¼ lb (115g) tomatoes (skinned and de-seeded), a finely-chopped green pepper (with the seeds removed) and ¼ lb (115g) cold cooked peas. Diced cooked ham or tongue or chicken may be added if liked.

Vegetable and Salad Dishes

FROM THE PAST

Gather the lettuces when they are going to seed, skin the stalks and cut them into pieces half the length of your finger; boil them slowly twenty minutes in a syrup made strong with powder ginger; the next day simmer them again; do this three or four days; let them stand in this syrup for a week or more if it does not mould, then strain them quite dry, and boil them two or three times in a thick syrup made strong with the best whole ginger. If this is done well it may be taken for the best India preserved ginger. (From *The Modern Cookery* by a Lady, published by J. and C. Mozley, London 1856.)

J. E. Morris, Piddletrenthide

Puddings

Una's Mother's Flaky Pastry
(This recipe comes from New Zealand)

8 oz (225g) self-raising flour   4 oz (115g) butter
1 teaspoon (4ml) vinegar   ½ cup (75ml) milk

Cut the butter finely into the flour, using a knife in each hand.
Mix to a dough with the milk into which you have added the
vinegar. Roll out three times, resting in between. Bake in a hot
oven.

Mrs M. D. Davidson, Piddlehinton

Rich Short Crust for Mince Pies

½ lb (225g) self-raising flour   1 egg yolk
Juice of half a lemon   1 teaspoon (4ml) caster sugar
4 oz (115g) butter   Pinch of salt

Rub butter into flour and sugar. Beat egg yolk with a little
water and mix all together. This pastry can be rolled very thin
and goes a long way. Bake in a moderately hot oven for about 35
minutes.

K. Clear, White Lackington

Lemon Fluff

2 oz (60g) semolina   2 lemons
¼ lb sugar (to taste)   16 oz (350ml) water

Sprinkle semolina carefully into cold water, stirring hard to
prevent lumps forming. Heat to boiling and boil for 6 minutes,
stirring occasionally. Pour into cold bowl, add lemon juice and
sugar. Whip. Leave to cool and then whip again hard until
mixture is white and frothy (use egg whisk or electric mixer and
whisk).

Clare Waddy, Piddletrenthide

Rum Russe

2 eggs
4 oz (115g) butter
4 oz (115g) caster sugar

4 tablespoons (80ml) rum
4 oz (115g) plain chocolate
1 packet of sponge fingers

Line a dish 6 inches (15cm) wide and 4 inches (10cm) deep (or a one-pint (575ml) pudding basin) with sponge fingers. Cream butter and sugar, adding egg yolks separately. Soften chocolate in basin over hot water – cool this and stir into mixture. Add 3 tablespoons rum. Mix well and add whipped egg whites. The remaining rum can be poured over the sponge fingers. Pour mixture into sponge finger 'mould' and leave in a refrigerator for a few hours to set. Turn out of dish carefully on to a plate. Decorate with cream, etc.

Mrs J. P. Andrew, Plush

Fruit Mousse

3 large eggs
1 egg yolk
4½ oz (130g) caster sugar
7½ fluid oz (170ml) purée
  (fruit)

½ oz (15g) gelatine
7½ fluid oz (170ml) double
  cream
Juice of small lemon

Put egg yolks and sugar in bowl and whisk over gentle heat until thick and mousse-like. Dissolve gelatine in lemon juice and add to egg mixture while hot. Add the fruit purée, whipped egg whites and whipped cream, when cool.

Noel Slade, Plush

Apple Jelly
(Serves 4)

1 lb (455g) cooking apples
½ pt (275ml) lemon jelly
3 oz (95g) granulated sugar

1 egg white
Rind of lemon

Peel, core and cut up apples and stew them with 2 tablespoons (40ml) water, sugar and the rind of lemon, stirring from time to time. When soft, rub through a sieve (or put in a liquidiser). Make jelly, using only half the usual quantity of water. When cold, mix with apple pulp and fold in the stiffly beaten egg white.

Sally Howard-Tripp, Piddletrenthide

Boodles Orange Fool
(Serves 6)

6 sponge cakes
¾ pt (425ml) double cream
4 oranges

Sugar to taste
2 lemons

Cut up sponge cakes lengthwise in slices and place in a glass dish. Put in a basin the grated rind of one lemon and two oranges and the juice of all the fruit. Mix with the cream and sugar to taste. Pour over the sponge cakes and allow to stand for at least six hours before serving.

Noel Slade, Plush

Helen's Pavlova (Marshmallow Meringue)
(This recipe comes from New Zealand)

4 egg whites	1 breakfast cup (275ml) caster
1 teaspoon (4ml) vinegar	sugar

Very lightly oil the type of plate that you can both bake on and send to the table. Whip egg whites to stiff peak. Whip in, very fast, $\frac{1}{3}$ of the sugar and continue to whip very fast for exactly 3 minutes. Then whip in more slowly and lightly the rest of the sugar alternately with the vinegar in drops. This will give you a firm and non-collapsible mixture. Pile and shape into a cake form on the oiled plate, making it about $\frac{2}{3}$ higher than you expect the finished cake. It will flatten in cooking. Bake on middle shelf of a 200°F, Gas Mark $\frac{1}{4}$ (110°C) oven for about $1\frac{1}{4}$ hours. Lower heat to 150°F (100°C) for last half hour. Cover with greaseproof paper if it seems to be over-colouring. Serve with fruit and cream dished separately.

Mrs M. D. Davidson, Piddlehinton

Golden Delight

1 slice bread (cut 1-inch thick)	2 tablespoons (40ml) milk
1 tablespoon (20ml) golden	Vanilla flavouring
syrup	2 oz (55g) butter

Remove the crust from the bread and round off the corners. Put milk flavoured with vanilla over the bread to soak it without making it sloppy. Melt the butter and the golden syrup together in a frying pan. When melted put in the bread and baste it well. Turn over and fry until crusty. Serve hot, with cream if desired.

Amy Till, Piddletrenthide

Great Grandmother's Christmas Pudding

6 oz (170g) self-raising flour
¾ lb (340g) stoned raisins
¼ lb (115g) mixed peel
2 oz (55g) almonds (skinned
    and chopped finely)
6 oz (170g) stale breadcrumbs
¾ lb (340g) currants (washed
    well and dried)
4 eggs

1 dessertspoon (10ml) mixed
    spice
12 oz (340g) suet (not packet
    suet) chopped finely
6 oz (170g) brown sugar
¼ pt (150ml) milk
¼ tumbler rum and brandy
    (mixed)

This is enough for two good-sized puddings. Mix all the dry ingredients together. Beat the eggs with the milk with ½ teaspoon (2ml) salt, add to the dry ingredients and mix well, then add the brandy and rum last and mix again. Put into well-greased pudding basins. Boil for 6½ hours, and 1½ hours on Christmas Day. If this recipe is strictly adhered to it makes a good dark and light pudding of excellent flavour.

Mrs R. Wright, Piddletrenthide

Lemon Flan
(Serves 4)

4 oz (115g) digestive biscuits
1 level tablespoon (20ml)
    caster sugar
2 oz (55g) butter

¼ pt (150ml) double cream
2 large lemons
6-oz (170g) can condensed
    milk

Crush biscuits with rolling pin. Melt butter, add sugar, then blend in biscuit crumbs, mix well. Turn mixture into a 7-inch (15cm) flan dish and press into shape round base and sides of dish. Bake in slow oven for 8 minutes. Remove from oven and leave to cool. Mix together cream, condensed milk and finely grated lemon rinds, slowly beat in lemon juice. Pour mixture into flan case and chill. Decorate with whipped cream.

Mrs C. R. Williams, Piddletrenthide

The Adaptable Pudding

2 lb (900g) self-raising flour   8 oz (225g) sugar
1 lb (455g) margarine

Rub the margarine into the flour until it looks like breadcrumbs.
Add the sugar and mix well. Store in a polythene bag in the
refrigerator. The mixture will keep well in the refrigerator for
about 2 months. Use as required, or as suggested below:

(1) For a steamed pudding, take 14 oz (395g) of the mixture, add
an egg and milk to make stiff dough. Add flavouring, e.g.
sultanas, marmalade, or put on to fruit, such as apples. Put into a
bowl and cover well. Boil for $1\frac{1}{2}$ hours.
(2) Use 9 oz (255g) of the mixture and use as for crumbles,
placing on fruit and baking at 400°F, Gas Mark 6 (200°C).
(3) Mix with water and use as a sweet pastry for fruit pies and
Dutch tarts.
(4) Mix some of the mixture with egg and add a small tin of fruit
(chop the fruit if necessary), making a stiff dough. Fry small
spoonfuls for 5–8 minutes on each side to make fruit fritters.
Serve with a fruit sauce.

Elizabeth Buchan, Piddletrenthide

Puddings

Pineapple Refrigerator Dessert

1 small can pineapple (crushed)   Digestive biscuit base
½ lb (225g) baby   ½ pt (275ml) whipping cream
  marshmallows

To make the digestive biscuit base: Crush 6 oz (170g) of
digestive biscuits finely and add 3 oz (95g) of melted margarine.
Reserve half a cup (90g). Use the rest to line a 9-inch (20cm) pie-
pan, pressing in firmly. Put in refrigerator to set until firm.
    Drain pineapple thoroughly. Heat the pineapple juice and melt
the marshmallows in the juice. Cool. Whip the cream and fold
into the marshmallow mixture. Add the pineapple. Pour over
base and sprinkle with reserved biscuit crumbs. Let stand to set,
preferably in the refrigerator.

Joan Potter, Piddletrenthide

Heavenly Pie

2 packets of sponge finger   Grated rind and juice of 1
  biscuits   lemon
¼ pt (150ml) white wine   1 tablespoon (20ml) raspberry
3 oz (95g) caster sugar   jam
½oz (15g) gelatine   Sliced lemon for decoration
2 oz (55g) butter, melted   ½ pt (275ml) double cream
3 tablespoons (60ml) water   Loose-based cake tin

Put aside approximately 17 biscuits for the sides. Crush the rest
in a polythene bag and add to the melted butter and press this
into the base of the tin. Spread one edge of each biscuit with jam
and arrange side by side round the inside of tin – sugar side out.
Mix wine, lemon rind and juice and sugar in a large bowl. Add
the cream and whisk until thick and fluffy. In a small pan,
sprinkle gelatine over the water and heat gently until dissolved –
then stir this into mixture. When almost set, pour into the tin.
Leave at least 1 hour in a cool place. Decorate with slice of lemon
and pipe more cream if desired.

Audrey Condon, Piddletrenthide

Economical Meringues

1 egg white
1 teaspoon (4ml) baking
    powder
6 oz (170g) granulated sugar

2 tablespoons (40ml) boiling
    water
1 teaspoon (4ml) vinegar

Beat white, sugar, water and vinegar until stiff. Add baking powder. Shape as required and bake in a simmering oven for 45 minutes. To prevent sticking to baking sheet wipe tin over with oil and cover with greaseproof paper. Oil paper slightly if necessary.

Mrs M. Walker, Plush

Mince Pie

8 oz (225g) flour
1 level teaspoon (4ml)
    powdered cinnamon
4 oz (115g) butter
1 whole egg

Mincemeat
2 oz (55g) *soft* brown sugar
⅓ gill (about 1 tablespoon,
    20ml) water, rather less
    than more

Sift flour on to board, making into a ring and into centre put sugar, butter (knifed up), cinnamon, egg and lastly water. Work well with fingers into smooth dough, taking care to catch water which tries to escape under flour. Knead, cover with a cloth and leave 24 hours. Roll out on floured board and put in flan tin, fill with mincemeat and cover with pastry. Make a slit in top of pastry. Don't give egg or milk wash. Bake in middle of oven at 450°F, Gas Mark 8 (230°C) for 30–40 minutes. Take out of oven and sift *thickly* with icing sugar.

Mrs E. Durham, Piddletrenthide

Puddings

Syllabub

¼ pt (150ml) white wine
2 tablespoons (40ml) lemon
  juice

½ pt (275ml) double cream
2 tablespoons (7ml) lemon rind
3 oz (95g) caster sugar

Whisk cream well and add other ingredients. Cool in refrigerator. Excellent with Christmas pudding.

Peggy Cake, Plush

Southcombe Syllabub
(Serves 6)

½ pt (275ml) double cream
4 oz (115g) loaf sugar
1 lemon (grated rind and juice)

½ glass sherry (to taste)
½ glass brandy (to taste)

Soak all but cream together for 1 to 2 hours. Whip cream well. Then add the soaked mixture, whipping all together until stiff. Serve in chilled individual glasses. Alternatively can be used as topping for lemon mousse, jelly, fruit pudding, etc.

Mrs Girdwood, Piddletrenthide

Ginger Nut Pudding
(Serves 6)

I was given this at Christmas time when the juice from a jar of preserved ginger was available. Quite excellent.

24 ginger nut biscuits
⅔ pt (300ml) whipping cream
Pieces of ginger

4 tablespoons (80ml) ginger
  juice (strong coffee or
  brandy are said to be
  alternatives)

Whip the cream – put some by for decorating. Sprinkle some ginger nuts with juice and place in dish. Cover with thin layer of cream. Then put on another layer of sprinkled biscuits and cream until all is used up, ending with biscuit. Put weighted plate on top and chill in refrigerator overnight. Next day, cover pudding

with the cream which was put by and decorate with some
chopped-up pieces of preserved ginger.

A. H. Waterfield, White Lackington

Paradise Pudding
(An 80-year-old recipe from my Grandmother)

3 eggs	Salt
3 apples	Nutmeg
¼ lb (115g) breadcrumbs	Rind of half a lemon and juice
3 oz (95g) sugar	of one lemon
3 oz (95g) currants	

Pare, core and mince the apples. Beat the eggs. Moisten the rest
of the ingredients with these and beat well. Put the pudding in a
buttered mould, tie it down with a cloth and boil 1½ hours.
Serve with sweet sauce.

Muriel Pike, Piddletrenthide

French Apple Tart

½ lb (225g) puff pastry	Rind of half a lemon
½ lb (225g) apples (peeled and	¼ pt (150ml) milk
grated)	2 oz (55g) butter
4 oz (115g) caster sugar	Beaten egg white
1 oz (30g) chopped almonds	

Line sandwich or oven-proof tart dish with pastry. Melt butter
in milk. Put sugar, lemon rind, apples and almonds together.
Add milk and butter and fold in beaten egg white. Prick pastry
case and pour in the apple mixture. Cook in a moderate oven for
½ hour.

Jane Gordon, Piddletrenthide

Margaret Wingfield Pudding
(So called because we first had it at her house)

Make a semolina pudding in a saucepan in the usual way with 2½ oz (70g) of semolina, 1 oz (30g) of sugar and a pint of milk. Cook for 5 minutes, then cool. Stir in 2 egg yolks and pour into a pie dish. Spread apple purée over the pudding and then the stiffly beaten egg whites. Cook in a fairly hot oven until the meringue is brown.

Muriel Pike, Piddletrenthide

Blackcurrant Brulée

Stew ½ lb (225g) blackcurrants and 3 oz (95g) soft brown sugar in ¼ pint (150ml) of water until cooked. Blend 1½ tablespoons (30ml) of arrowroot in 1 tablespoon (20ml) of water, stir this into the blackcurrants and continue cooking for a couple of minutes until the purée has thickened and cleared. Put in a fireproof serving dish and cool. Spread the contents of a 5-oz carton of sour cream over the top and sprinkle enough soft brown sugar over the cream to cover it. Add a pinch of cinnamon and flash under the grill until the cream and sugar are brown and bubbling. Refrigerate. Blackberry and apple purée can be used instead of blackcurrants if preferred.

Christmas Cream

Melt 8 oz (225g) plain chocolate in a pan over hot water. Beat in 1 oz (30g) softened butter and 2 egg yolks. Break up 15 oz (425g) chestnut purée (from a tin) with a fork and beat into the chocolate. Add 3 dessertspoons (30ml) brandy and a teaspoon (2ml) of instant coffee dissolved in 2 teaspoons (7ml) of hot water. Sweeten with icing sugar. Whip ½ pint (275ml) double cream and fold in. Turn into a bowl or individual dishes and chill.

Green Dragon Cream
(Serves 8)

¼ pt (275ml) sweet cider
4 tablespoons (80ml) sherry
6 oz (170g) sugar

1 pt (575ml) double cream
8 tablespoons (150ml)
  sweetened apple purée

Leave the sugar soaking in the sherry for 2 hours. Add the cream and whisk until thick. Put a spoonful of apple purée in the bottom of a sundae glass and pour the syllabub on top. Chill.

Doris Moore, The Green Dragon, Piddletrenthide

Banana Cream
(Serves 4 – 6)

10 bananas
2 oz (55g) sugar

⅓ cup (75ml) cream
1 lemon

Peel bananas, cut into slices. Put into saucepan, add the sugar and a little water. Cook until soft (about 15 minutes), turning continually. Beat into pulp. Cool in refrigerator or freezer. Add the juice of the lemon and the lightly whipped cream. Serve in dish or individual bowls.

A. H. Waterfield, White Lackington

Strawberry Mousse
(Serves 12 – 14)

2 level teaspoons (7ml)
  gelatine
½ pt (275ml) strawberry purée
  (fresh or frozen)

1 large tin evaporated milk
2 level tablespoons (40ml)
  sugar

Whip the chilled milk until thick. Add the purée, the gelatine
dissolved in one tablespoon of water and the sugar. Whip until
mixed. Pour into sundae glasses and decorate.

Alternative: Coffee nut mousse

Omit purée. Dissolve 1 level dessertspoon (10ml) of coffee
powder in 4 tablespoons (80ml) water. Make as above adding 2
oz (55g) mixed nuts before pouring into glasses

Blackcurrant Cheese Cake

4 oz (115g) cream cheese
4 oz (115g) icing sugar
6 oz (170g) digestive biscuits

½ pt (275ml) cream
Tin of blackcurrant pie filling
3 oz (95g) butter

Line loose-bottomed 8-inch (18cm) cake tin with the biscuit
crust (crumbled biscuits mixed with the melted butter). Mix the
cream cheese and icing sugar together and add most of the
whipped cream. Place on top of the biscuit crust, leave to set for
a while and then spread the blackcurrant pie filling on top and
decorate with the rest of the cream.

Audrey Condon, Piddletrenthide

Lemon Foam

Separate 4 eggs and whisk the yolks with 6 oz (170g) sugar. Into
this grate the rinds of 2 lemons. Dissolve a 2-oz (55g) packet of
powdered gelatine in the lemon juice over a gentle heat. Pour
this into the egg and sugar mixture gradually, whisking all the
time. Whisk the egg whites until stiff and fold into the mixture.

Pour into a bowl or individual dishes and chill.

Muriel Pike, Piddletrenthide

Orchard Delight
(A good way of using up a glut of fallen apples)

1 lb (455g) sweetened apple
  purée
2 cups (360g) breadcrumbs
1 oz (30g) sugar

1 oz (30g) butter
2 oz (55g) chocolate
¼ pt (150ml) whipped cream

Fry the breadcrumbs and sugar in the butter until brown and crisp. Place alternate layers of crumbs and apple purée in a serving dish, starting and finishing with the crumbs. When quite cold, pile the whipped cream on top and finish with a sprinkling of chocolate.

Five-Minute Lemon Meringue

1 flan case made with
  short crust pastry
6 oz (170g) sugar
1 lemon

2 eggs
1 tablespoon (20ml) cornflour
½ pt (275ml) water

Cut the lemon in quarters and liquidise with 3 oz (95g) of the sugar, the egg yolk, the cornflour and the water. Strain into a pan, add the butter and cook until it thickens. Cool and then fill the flan case with the mixture. Stiffly whisk the egg whites with 1 oz (30g) of the sugar. Fold in the remaining sugar and whisk again. Pile the meringue on top of the filling, dredge with a little sugar and put in a fairly hot oven until the meringue is a golden-brown.

Puddings

Chocolate Leaves

Wash and dry sturdy rose leaves, leaving a small stem. Paint melted chocolate on back of each leaf quite thickly. Put in the refrigerator to set. Peel off leaves with the point of a knife. Use to decorate special cakes and puddings.

John Firrell, Piddletrenthide

Summer Pudding
(The old country favourite for use with raspberries, currants, blackberries, etc.)

Line a greased basin with thin slices of bread, buttered both sides (stale bread may be used for this). Heat the chosen fruit (one kind or a mixture) with sugar until tender. Pour half into the lined basin, cover with a further slice of bread and butter, add the rest of the fruit and top with more bread and butter. Put a saucer on top, with a heavy weight on this. Refrigerate. Turn into a bowl and serve with whipped cream.

Peach Caramels
(Serves 5)

5 peaches
¼ pt (150ml) whipped cream (sweetened)
1 cupful (180g) soft brown sugar
2 tablespoons (40ml) milk
1 tablespoon (20ml) butter
Chopped nuts for garnish
Ice cream for accompaniment

Stand peaches in boiling water for 2 minutes. Drop into cold water, rub gently with fingers to remove skins, stand on a flat plate to drain and cool. Carefully cut in halves and remove the stones. Fill peach centres with whipped cream (save some for topping). Join halves together, secure with cocktail sticks. Put sugar, milk and butter in a saucepan, stir until boiling and simmer for 7 minutes. Beat until beginning to thicken, and then pour over the peaches. When cold, remove the cocktail sticks.

Top each with a swirl of cream and sprinkle with chopped nuts.

Jill Uht, Piddletrenthide

Ginger and Pear Fluff
(Serves 2)

1 small tin sliced pears
  in syrup
1 level teaspoon (4ml)
  gelatine
Rind of $\frac{1}{2}$ small lemon,
  grated

$1\frac{1}{2}$ oz (45g) ginger biscuits,
  crushed
2 tablespoons (40ml) double
  cream
1 egg white

Drain pears, retaining syrup. Rub pears through sieve and stir in
2 tablespoons (40ml) of the syrup. Dissolve gelatine in 2 more
tablespoons (40ml) of the syrup over hot water. Stir dissolved
gelatine and lemon rind into the pears and leave in a cold place
until starting to set. Whisk together the cream and a further
teaspoon (4ml) of the syrup until thick. Whisk egg white until
thick. With a metal spoon, fold the whisked cream and egg
white and the ginger biscuits into the pear mixture. Leave until
set.

Alison Pike, Piddletrenthide and Oxford

'Let's Get Rid of the Christmas Cake'

Christmas cake
Sherry or brandy
Frozen raspberries

3 eggs and $\frac{1}{2}$ pt (275ml)
  cream mixed together
Demerara sugar

Put crumbled slice of cake into individual ramekin dishes, with a
dash of sherry or brandy on each. Pour on egg and cream
mixture. Bake for 20 minutes at 375°F, Gas Mark 5 (190°C).
Cool. Cover with layer of raspberries and thick layer of demerara
sugar. Caramelise under very hot grill.

Jillie Edwards, Piddletrenthide

Lemon/Orange Sorbet

Juice of 1 lemon
Grated rind and juice of 1
 orange
6 oz (170g) sugar
2 tablespoons (40ml) golden
 syrup

$\frac{3}{4}$ pt (425ml) water
4 mint leaves or pinch of dried
 mint
1 egg white
1 oz (30g) sugar

Put sugar, $\frac{1}{4}$ pint (150ml) water and mint into pan and stir over a low heat until dissolved. Strain and then stir in $\frac{1}{2}$ pint (275ml) water, lemon juice, orange rind and juice and golden syrup. Mix well and pour into a container and freeze for about one hour or until half frozen. Beat egg white until stiff and add sugar. Pour half-frozen fruit mixture into a bowl and whisk, then gently stir in the egg white. Return to container, mix with rest of half-frozen fruit, and freeze.

I usually double this amount. It makes a very refreshing sweet after a large meal.

Pineapple Sorbet

3 lemons, thinly peeled
1 pt (575ml) water
9 oz (295g) caster sugar

1 medium-sized fresh
 pineapple
2 egg whites

Place lemon peelings with sugar and water in a pan and melt slowly until the sugar has dissolved. Bring to the boil and simmer for 10 minutes. Pour $\frac{1}{4}$ pint (150ml) fresh juice slowly into mixture. Add one teaspoonful (4ml) lemon juice. Pour the mixture into an ice tray and freeze. Whisk two egg whites and fold into the frozen mixture in a bowl. Return to the freezer and freeze until solid. Dice the fresh pineapple. Scoop the sorbet into glasses and top with chunks of fruit. Allow to defrost slightly before serving as this brings out the flavour more.

Joan Chandler, Brace of Pheasants, Plush

Lemon Solid
(This recipe has been handed down by word of mouth
in the family for four generations)

6 oz (170g) caster sugar 1 pt (575ml) fresh milk
2 lemons (preferably not pasteurised)
½ oz (15g) gelatine

Place the finely grated lemon rind in a 1½-pint (850ml) basin.
Add ½ pint (275ml) of milk to the sugar and rind. Squeeze the
lemon juice and set aside. Heat the remaining ½ pint (275ml) of
milk with the gelatine, being careful *not* to boil the milk. Add
the heated milk to the cold milk, stirring gently to dissolve the
sugar. Add the lemon juice (don't be alarmed if the milk appears
to curdle). Pour into a mould which has been rinsed in cold
water. Allow to stand in a cold larder for at least 12 hours.
Remove from the mould. The pudding should have separated,
with a clear jelly on top and 'curds' at the bottom.

Marion Wightman, Piddletrenthide

The Empress's Rice
(Simple but delicious – not at all like rice pudding!)
(Serves 5)

Boil 1⅓ pints (750ml) and ½ teacup (90g) rice together for ¾
hour. Dissolve 2 packets gelatine in some milk with 4
soupspoons (40ml) fine sugar. Mix all together and leave to cool.
When cold pour in ½ pint (275ml) whipped cream, mix well and
tip into a mould. (Some glacé mixed fruits may be added.) Cool
well in the refrigerator. Before serving, tip out on to a dish and
garnish with more glacé fruit.

A. H. Waterfield, White Lackington

Puddings

Christmas Pudding in the Arctic
(If you are fed up with the inevitable plum pudding
at Christmas, try this)

5 egg yolks
5 oz (145g) sugar
3 level tablespoons (60ml)
   tinned chestnut purée
4 oz (115g) plain chocolate
½ pt (275ml) double cream
½ pt (275ml) single cream

4 tablespoons (80ml) rum or
   brandy
3 oz (95g) mixed dried fruit
   (sultanas, currants and
   chopped raisins)
2 oz (55g) mixed peel
1 oz (30g) glacé cherries

Soak the dried fruit, peel and cherries in the rum until
thoroughly marinaded. Heat the single cream until it is almost
boiling and then pour it over the egg yolks and sugar. Return to
a double saucepan (or a basin over hot water) and stir until it
thickens. Then add the chestnut purée and chocolate. Stir until
all is melted and dissolved. Cool and then fold in the dried fruit
and rum. Finally fold in the stiffly whipped double cream. Turn
into a basin lined with foil, and freeze. When frozen, it can be
removed from the basin, wrapped in the foil and returned to the
freezer. Defrost for about 2 hours before serving.

Muriel Pike, Piddletrenthide

Dorset Dumplings

Suet crust
½ lb (225g) self-raising flour
Pinch of salt

¼ lb (115g) suet,
   grated or chipped finely

Sieve flour and salt, add suet. Make fairly stiff dough with cold
water.

Filling
4 small cooking apples
½ lb (225g) demerera sugar
¼ lb (115g) butter or margerine

2 teaspoons (7ml) ground ginger
1 wineglassful rum
Cloves

Peel apples and remove cores without breaking the fruit. Roll out the pastry and cut into pieces large enough to cover the apples. Mix together the sugar, butter, ginger and rum. Place an apple in the centre of each piece of pastry, fill up the hollow with the rum mixture, piling it well on top. Press in 1 clove, fold over the pastry, wetting edges well. Press edges firmly together to keep the mixture inside. Put each dumpling in a well-floured cloth, drop into boiling water and boil for 45 mintues – or steam for about 1 hour.

Jill Uht, Piddletrenthide

Bramble Bombe

Purée

1 lb (455g) blackberries	A little water
4 oz (115g) sugar	

Place in a saucepan, cover and cook gently until fruit is soft. Cool slightly. Rub fruit through a sieve. Makes approximately 1 pint (575ml).

$\frac{1}{4}$ pt (150ml) double cream	2 handfuls broken meringue
$\frac{1}{4}$ pt (150ml) single cream	

Measure $\frac{1}{2}$ pint (275ml) of the purée (keep the rest for sauce) Whip creams until fluffy and fold in meringue pieces. Add the purée very carefully, folding into the cream and meringue mixture. Do not overfold. It should have a marbled effect. Put into a 2-pint (1.15l) basin and freeze. When ready to serve, dip basin into handhot water and turn on to plate. Spoon a little of the reserved purée over the top and serve the rest separately. If a softer texture is required, put into the fridge an hour before serving.

Cakes, Biscuits and Bread

Great-Grandfather's Christmas Cake
(Keep one or two months)

$\frac{1}{2}$ lb (225g) fresh butter
1$\frac{1}{2}$ lb (680g) currants
$\frac{1}{4}$ lb (115g) ground almonds
$\frac{1}{2}$ lb (225g) caster sugar
10 oz (280g) self-raising flour

1 level teaspoon (225g) mixed
   spice
5 new-laid eggs
$\frac{1}{4}$ lb (115g) mixed peel

Put butter in basin and melt in oven. Add sugar and eggs, one by one, beating up well between each, then add fruit and flour. Bake in a moderate oven (325°F, Gas Mark 3 or 170°C) for about 4 hours.

Heather Parry, Piddletrenthide

Dorset Apple Cake

Recipe 1

4 oz (115g) margarine
6 oz (170g) self-raising flour
4 oz (115g) caster sugar

1 lb (455g) cooking apples
2 eggs
A few sultanas or raisins

Cream fat and sugar, add the eggs, then the flour. Slice the apples and add to the mixture with the dried fruit. Put in a greased tin and cook in a moderate oven (325°F, Gas Mark 3 or 170°C) until a golden colour and firm to the touch. When the cake is cool, mix 2 oz (95g) butter and 2 oz (95g) soft brown sugar. Spread on the cake or place in little heaps.

Recipe 2

2 oz (95g) bread crumbs
1 orange
2 oz (95g) butter

2 oz (95g) sugar
1 lb (455g) cooking apples

Cook apples with juice of orange until tender. Put in a greased pie dish. Melt butter in a saucepan, add breadcrumbs and sugar, add grated rind of orange, and put on top of apple. Cook until breadcrumbs are a lovely golden brown.

Mrs Paul, Piddletrenthide

Yeast Cake

Cream together ½ lb (225g) butter and ½ lb (225g) sugar. Add 2 well-beaten eggs. Add ½ lb (225g) currants, ½ lb (225g) sultanas, ¼ lb (115g) candied peel and grated nutmeg. Mix well. Add 4 teacups (720g) flour, 2 teaspoons (7ml) baking powder, ½ pint (275ml) warm milk and ½ oz (15g) yeast. Lastly add ½ teaspoon (2ml) bicarbonate of soda mixed in 1 tablespoon (20ml) of vinegar. Mix thoroughly. Line a tin with buttered paper and put in cake mixture. Allow cake to rise for 1 hour in a warm place. Bake in a moderate oven for 2 hours.

Heather Parry, Piddletrenthide

Lemon Cake

5 oz (145g) self-raising flour	Rind and juice of ½ lemon
2 tablespoons (40ml) lemon curd	4 oz (115g) soft margarine
4 oz (115g) caster sugar	2 eggs

Rub all ingredients together, then add eggs. Bake ¾ hour 350°F, Gas Mark 4 (180°C). Then ¼ hour 300°F, Gas Mark 2.

Topping (To be carefully spooned over hot cake)
2 tablespoons (40ml) granulated sugar, rind and juice of 1 lemon.

Una's Caramel Cake
(This recipe comes from New Zealand)

¼ lb (115g) butter	1 egg
½ cup (90g) dates	½ cup (90g) chopped walnuts
Few drops essence of vanilla and essence of ginger	1 small teaspoon (3ml) baking powder
¼ lb (115g) soft brown sugar	1 cup (180g) flour

Cream butter and sugar, beat in flour, egg and essences. Add fruit and nuts. Spread in shallow square tin, and bake for 20-25 minutes at 350°F, Gas Mark 4 (180°C). Have ready: 2 teaspoons (7ml) golden syrup, 2 oz (95g) butter, 4 oz (115g) icing sugar, essence of ginger. Boil all together gently for 1 minute and spread over top of cake while hot.

Mrs M. D. Davidson, Piddlehinton

Anne's Chocolate Cake
(This recipe comes from New Zealand)

¼ lb (115g) butter
1 dessertspoon (10ml) golden syrup
1 teaspoon (4ml) baking soda
1 small cup (180g) sugar
1½ cups (270g) flour

1 tablespoon (20ml) cocoa
1 egg
1 teaspoon (4ml) baking powder
1 cup milk

Cream butter and sugar. Beat in egg and syrup. Sift baking powder and soda into flour and add to creamed mixture alternately with milk. Spread into buttered tin and bake in hot oven (400–425°F, Gas Mark 6–7 or 200–220°C) about half an hour.

Icing

1 oz (30g) butter
4 oz (115g) icing sugar
1 tablespoon (20ml) cocoa

1 dessertspoon (10ml) hot water

Boil quickly together until blended and melted, and spread on cake.

Mrs M. D. Davidson, Piddlehinton

Jumble Cake

4 oz (115g) self-raising flour
5 oz (145g) margarine
2 oz (55g) chopped walnuts
4 oz (115g) ground hazelnuts
4 oz (115g) sugar
3 eggs

2 oz (55g) fruit (cherries,
crystallized ginger,
pineapple, angelica, etc.)
4-oz (115g) block of milk
chocolate

Cream margarine and sugar. Add each egg separately with a little flour, and cream. Finally mix in remainder of flour, chopped chocolate, nuts and fruit. Line tin with greaseproof paper and cook as for fruit cake 1½ to 2 hours at 300°F.

Miss W. Murrell, Plush

Viennese Biscuit Cake

2 oz (55g) butter
½ lb (225g) digestive biscuits
4½ oz (130g) plain chocolate

2 tablespoons (40ml) golden
syrup

Crumble biscuits, not too finely. Place remaining ingredients in a small heavy pan over low heat and allow to dissolve completely. Stir in crumbs to a smooth paste and press into an oiled flan ring standing on oiled baking sheet. Smooth the top with the cut side of an orange or lemon. When partly set mark into slices. When quite set remove from ring, wrap in foil and keep in refrigerator.

Mrs M. D. Davidson, Piddlehinton

Dorset Blackcurrant Cake

8 oz (225g) flour
8 oz (225g) blackcurrants (or
more)

4 oz (115g) butter
4 oz (115g) sugar

Cream butter and sugar, add flour. Mix with milk and water and then add blackcurrants. Put mixture in fairly flat tins and cook in a moderate oven.

Mrs V. Ralph, Alton Pancras

Irish Sponge Cake

3 eggs
1 tablespoon (20ml) lemon
   juice and rind

6 oz (170g) caster sugar
4 oz (115g) plain white flour

Beat eggs, add sugar and beat until thick and creamy. Stir in lemon juice and grated rind and sifted flour. Sift a little caster sugar on top of cake in tin. Bake in oven 350°F, Gas Mark 3 (170°C) for about 50 minutes. Cool slowly and allow to become nearly cold before turning out of tin.

Noel Slade, Plush

Cut and Come Again Cake

12 oz (340g) self-raising flour
2 oz (55g) dripping
2 oz (55g) margarine
6 oz (170g) sugar

2 oz (55g) lard
1 egg and a little milk
6 oz (170g) sultanas and
   cherries, mixed

Rub fat into flour. Add the other ingredients and the egg broken (not beaten). Add sufficient milk to make a stiff dough. Put into greased tin and sprinkle top with sugar. Bake in oven 400°F, Gas Mark 5 (190°C) to start with and then 350°F, Gas Mark 4 (180°C) for 1 to 1¼ hours. For a richer cake use 2 eggs and more fat.

Jane Gordon, Piddletrenthide

Dorset Soda Cake

1 lb (455g) flour
Salt
½ lb (225g) currants
1 small teaspoon (4ml)
  bicarbonate of soda
¾ lb (340g) margarine

½ pt (275ml) boiling milk
½ lb (225g) sultanas
½ lb (225g) sugar
3 eggs
A little nutmeg and peel if
  liked

Break down margarine into the flour and salt and work it into small crumbs. Mix these well with the sugar. Stir in the boiling milk and then add the well-whisked eggs. Add nutmeg and peel (if liked) and then the currants and sultanas. Beat well together and lastly add bicarbonate of soda (dissolved in a little milk). Bake for 2 hours in a moderate oven. A very good moist cake.

Mrs V. Ralph, Alton Pancras

Piddle Apple Cake

¾ lb (340g) self-raising flour
2 eggs
A good pinch of salt
½ lb (225g) margarine or
  butter

4 large good cooking apples
½ lb (225g) sugar (light brown
  or demerara)
A good pinch of mixed spice

Mix well all dry ingredients and margarine. Peel and grate apples on large grater and add to mixture. Beat eggs with a little milk and add to other ingredients. Beat to make a fairly loose mixture. Cook in oven at 400°F, Gas Mark 6 (200°C) until golden brown. Serve hot or cold with cream or custard.

Mrs N. Baker, Piddletrenthide

Boiled Fruit Cake

1 lb (455g) mixed fruit
2 eggs
2 teacups (360g) self-raising
flour
5 oz (145g) margarine

1 teacup (150ml) water
1 teaspoon (4ml) bicarbonate
of soda
1 teacup (180g) sugar

Put fruit, water, sugar and margarine into saucepan and stir slowly until fat melts. Add bicarbonate and boil for 20 minutes. Leave several hours or overnight, then add beaten eggs and flour. Place in a lined 7 inches (15cm) by 3 inches (9cm) tin and bake at 310°F, Gas Mark 2 (150°C) for two hours.

Kathy Jakeman, Piddletrenthide

Cake To Keep

This cake will keep fresh for several months if you put it in a tin; in fact, it is nicest when kept a little before cutting. Cream together $\frac{1}{2}$ lb (225g) each of sugar and butter. Sift in $\frac{1}{2}$ lb (225g) of flower [she could never spell!]. Add a few blanched and chopped almonds, $\frac{1}{2}$ lb (225g) each of currants and raisins and 3 well-beaten eggs. Finally mix in half a wineglassfull of brandy.

Christine, age 10

Dorset Cider Cake

8 oz (225g) butter	1 teaspoon (4ml) bicarbonate
12 oz (340g) flour	of soda
1 teaspoon (4ml) ground	Grated rind of one orange
cinnamon	3 eggs
1 teaspoon (4ml) baking	6 fluid oz (160ml) cider
powder	2-inch (5cm) piece of candied
4 oz (115g) sugar	orange peel cut into strips

Lightly grease an 8-inch (18cm) cake tin. Sift together flour, cinnamon, baking powder and soda. Cream butter until soft. Add sugar and orange rind. Beat until mixture is light and fluffy. Beat in eggs, one at a time, adding a tablespoon (20ml) of flour mixture with each egg. Beat in remaining flour mixture. Pour in cider slowly, beating constantly with a spoon. When batter is smooth and thoroughly combined, spoon into prepared tin. Arrange strips of peel over the batter. Bake for $1\frac{1}{4}$ to $1\frac{1}{2}$ hours. Oven temperature 325°F, Gas Mark 3 (170°C).

John Firrell, Piddletrenthide

The Original Dorset Apple Dough Cake

There is no written recipe for this. The dough was bought from the village baker, the cake made and returned to be cooked in the bakehouse oven, fetched when cooked and eaten hot for tea.

As many sliced apples as possible were mixed into a bread dough. This was spread on an enamel or fireproof plate and baked. When cooked, the cake was split in half and spread with butter and sugar. It was always eaten hot.

Marion Wightman, Piddletrenthide

Ginger Parkin

6 oz (170g) self-raising flour
1 level teaspoon (4ml)
 bicarbonate of soda
2 oz (55g) fat
1 oz (30g) sugar

1–2 teaspoons (4–7ml) ground
 ginger (or chocolate)
2 tablespoons (20ml) syrup
Pinch of salt

Put dry ingredients into bowl and rub in fat, add syrup and a little milk if necessary. Mix, and bake in a moderate oven for 40 minutes.

Heather Parry, Piddletrenthide

Swedish Biscuits
(The Wonder)

6 oz (170g) oatmeal
5-6 oz (145-170g) butter
4 oz (115g) sugar
4 oz (115g) plain flour

3 oz (95g) raisins
1 small teaspoon (4ml)
 bicarbonate of soda

Cream sugar and butter. Work in dry ingredients. Roll in hands. Bake in oven 350°F, Gas Mark 4 to 5 until crisp — about 20 minutes.

Granthams
(Biscuits)

2 oz (55g) margarine
¼ teaspoon (1ml) bicarbonate
   of soda
4 oz (115g) caster sugar
About 1 dessertspoon (10ml)
   beaten egg
4 oz (115g) flour

1 teaspoon (4ml) ginger or
   chocolate powder
Few drops of vanilla or ½
   teaspoon (2ml) of powdered
   cinnamon may be added to
   the chocolate variety

Cream the margarine and half the sugar until light, add the remaining sugar and cream again. Sieve flour, ginger and soda together. Add this to the cream alternately with the egg making the mixture just moist enough to roll into balls the size of ping pong balls. Place well apart on greased baking tin. Put in the oven at 350°F, Gas Mark 4 (180°C). Let oven drop at once to 325°F, Gas Mark 3 (170°C). Bake about 20 minutes until firm.

Miss W. Murrell, Plush

Flapjacks

3 oz (95g) soft brown sugar
1 tablespoon (20ml) golden
   syrup

4 oz (115g) quick porridge
   oats
3 oz (95g) butter

Put brown sugar and butter into a saucepan and melt very gently. Do not let mixture boil. Remove from heat and add porridge oats and golden syrup, stirring thoroughly with a wooden spoon. Grease a sandwich tin. Put the mixture into the tin, spreading it evenly. Bake in moderate oven (350°F, Gas Mark 4 or 180°C) until beginning to turn brown, usually 15-20 minutes. Leave to cool and cut into fingers.

Georgina Geffers, Piddletrenthide

Melting Moments

8 oz (225g) soft margarine
2 tablespoons (40ml) cocoa
4 oz (115g) caster sugar

Pinch of salt
8 oz (225g) plain flour

Place everything in bowl. Mix together with electric mixer.
Roll into balls. Cover with rolled oats. Place on greased baking
tin. Flatten slightly with fork. Cook at 375°F, Gas Mark 5
(190°C) for 10-15 minutes.

Kathy Jakeman, Piddletrenthide

Tea Bread

1 cup (150ml) cold tea
2 cups (360g) self-raising flour
1 cup (180g) fruit

Spice if liked
$\frac{1}{2}$ cup (90g) demerara sugar

Soak tea, fruit and sugar overnight. Stir in flour and cook for
about $\frac{3}{4}$ to 1 hour at 375°F, Gas Mark 5 (190°C) in well-greased
loaf tin. Make sure you use the same sized cup for all the
ingredients. Serve hot with butter.

Mrs Christine Abbott, Piddletrenthide

Belgian Loaf

1 cup (180g) sugar
2 cups (360g) plain flour
$\frac{1}{2}$ teaspoon (2ml) bicarbonate
    of soda
1 cup (150ml) milk

4 oz (115g) margarine
1 egg
1 cup (180g) sultanas
$\frac{1}{2}$ teaspoon (2ml) baking
    powder

Put sugar, sultanas, milk and margarine in a saucepan and bring
slowly to the boil stirring well. Leave to cool and then add dry
ingredients and egg. Beat well. Put into a greased loaf tin and
cook for one hour on middle shelf (355°F, Gas Mark 4 or
180°C).

Kate Shea, Piddletrenthide

Balmoral Scones

½ lb (225g) plain flour
1 teaspoon (4ml) cream of
  tartar
1 egg
Good pinch of salt

1½ oz (45g) margarine
About half a cupful milk
½ teaspoon (2ml) bicarbonate
  of soda
1 tablespoon (20ml) sugar

Mix together the flour, salt, bicarbonate of soda and cream of
tartar. Rub in the fat and add the sugar. Make into a stiff dough
with the egg and milk, reserving a little of the egg for brushing
over the tops of the scones. Roll out, cut into small rounds
about half an inch (1cm) thick, and place on a floured tin. Brush
with egg, and bake in a good oven for from 12 to 15 minutes —
400°F or Gas Mark 6 (200°C). These were Queen Victoria's
favourite scones.

Mrs Chanter, Alton Pancras

Caramel Squares

Shortbread

6 oz (170g) soft margarine
3 oz (95g) caster sugar

7½ oz (200g) plain flour

Cream together the sugar and margarine. Stir in the flour and
knead. Press into a tin 10-inch (20cm) by 5-inch (10cm) and bake
for 15 to 20 minutes at 350°F, Gas Mark 4 (180°C).

Filling

4 oz (115g) margarine
Small tin condensed milk
4 oz (115g) soft brown sugar

2 tablespoons (40ml) syrup
1 teaspoon (4ml) vanilla
  essence

Place all the ingredients in a small pan. Bring to the boil stirring
all the time and simmer for approximately 5 minutes until the
toffee comes away from the sides of the pan. Pour over the
shortbread and leave to cool.

Topping

4 oz (115g) plain cooking chocolate melted in a basin over hot water. Pour over the toffee and when cold cut into small squares.

Elizabeth Larpent, Piddlehinton

Great Grandmother Bennett's Ginger Biscuits
(Suitable for a church tea party)

3 lb (1.35K) plain flour	6 oz (170g) almonds, shredded
1½ lb (680g) butter or	or chopped
margarine	1½ oz (45g) ground ginger
1½ lb (680g) caster sugar	3 teaspoons (95g) bicarbonate
6 oz (170g) chopped peel	of soda
(finely shredded cap peel is	1 teaspoon (30g) cinnamon
best)	1 lb 2 oz (510g) treacle

Rub fat into flour. Add all other dry ingredients. Work to a stiff dough with the syrup (hands are best). Shape into balls the size of walnuts, 4 to a greased tray. Put in oven to warm through (3–4 minutes). Remove and flatten with tips of fingers. Return to oven and bake until dark golden brown (about 8–10 minutes) at 400°F, Gas Mark 6 (200°C). Cool on wire tray.

If possible have about 4 Swiss roll size tins in use. The biscuits will keep six weeks in an airtight tin. 1 lb of flour makes 72 biscuits.

Ruth Read, Piddlehinton

Dorset Easter Biscuits

1 lb (455g) plain flour	¾ lb (340g) soft margarine
3 egg yolks	½ lb (225g) caster sugar
3 oz (95g) currants	Spice (optional)

Mix all ingredients (with electric mixer if possible). Roll out thinly, cut into rounds, prick well and bake 15–20 minutes (350°F, Gas Mark 4 or 180°C). (N.B. Use the egg whites to make meringues. They will keep for weeks in an airtight container.)

Ginger and Peach Gâteau

1 bought ginger cake   1 small tin peaches
Small pot double cream   Chocolate for decoration
1 teaspoon (4ml) sugar

Cut the ginger cake in half and lay halves side by side on serving dish. Spoon over about 3 to 4 tablespoons (60-80ml) of the peach juice until the cake is fairly moist. Whip the double cream with the sugar until fairly thick (saving a little for decoration). Cover the cake with the cream, place the peaches on top and decorate with the rest of the cream and chocolate leaves or triangles. This is a very quick and attractive sweet.

Black Cherry and Chocolate Gâteau
(Serves 8–10)

1 chocolate sponge $\frac{1}{2}$ pt (275ml) double cream
1 tin of black cherry pie filling   Chocolate for decoration

Make the chocolate sponge preferably in an 8-inch (15cm) tin. When cold cut it in half. Whip the cream with a little sugar (saving some for piping decoration). Spread some of the cream over the bottom half of the cake and then spread the pie filling on top. Then cover with a little more cream. Place the top half of the cake on it, spread over the rest of the cream and decorate with chocolate curls.

Peanut Fingers

4 oz (115g) demerara sugar   3 oz (95g) desiccated coconut
4 oz (115g) butter   2 oz (55g) sultanas
2 eggs   2 oz (55g) peanuts, chopped
6 oz (170g) self-raising flour   Vanilla essence to taste

Cream the sugar and butter. Add the beaten eggs, one at a time. Fold in the sifted flour, coconut, sultanas and peanuts and lastly a few drops of vanilla essence. Turn into a square greased pan and smooth the top. Bake in a moderate oven for about ¾ hour. Cool. Sift a little icing sugar over the top and cut into fingers.

Chocolate Fudge Fingers

4 oz (115g) butter or margarine
2 tablespoons (40ml) golden syrup
8 oz (225g) crushed sweet biscuits

1 oz (30g) raisins or mixed fruit
2 oz (55g) quartered glacé cherries
5 oz (145g) plain chocolate, broken into small pieces

Grease and line a small flat tin. Melt the butter and syrup in a saucepan and stir in the biscuits, fruit, cherries and chopped chocolate. Press firmly into the tin and chill in the refrigerator until set. Cut into small fingers.

Alison Pike, Piddletrenthide and Oxford

Mincemeat Cookies

2 oz (55g) sugar
3 oz (95g) soft margarine
1 tablespoon (20ml) milk
1 beaten egg

4 oz (115g) self-raising flour
2 tablespoons (40ml) mincemeat

Mix together sugar and margarine. Add egg, beat well and then add the flour and milk followed by the mincemeat. Place in well-greased patty tins. Bake at 375°F, Gas Mark 5 (190°C) for 14 minutes.

Ann Matthews, Piddletrenthide

Cherry Nibbles

Grease a Swiss roll tin and line with greaseproof paper. Melt 5 oz (145g) chocolate and spread over bottom of tin. Allow to cool. Mix 4 oz (115g) coconut, 4 oz (115g) caster sugar, 2 oz (55g) chopped glacé cherries, 2 oz (55g) sultanas and 2 beaten eggs. Spread this over the chocolate and bake for $\frac{1}{2}$ hour on middle shelf at 345°F, Gas Mark 4 (180°C). Allow to cool and cut into fingers.

Coconut Slices

8 oz (225g) short crust pastry	4 oz (115g) coconut
Jam	2 oz (55g) ground rice
4 oz (115g) sugar	2 eggs
4 oz (115g) icing sugar	

Line Swiss roll tin with pastry and cover this with jam. Mix dry ingredients together and bind with beaten eggs. Spread this mixture over the jam. Sprinkle top with nuts if liked. Bake in a hot oven (420°F, Gas Mark 7 or 220°C) for about 25 mintues. Cut into fingers when cold.

Bondakor
(A Danish biscuit)

$3\frac{1}{2}$ oz (110g) margarine	7 oz (185g) flour
$3\frac{1}{2}$ oz (110g) sugar	$\frac{1}{2}$ teaspoon (2 ml) bicarbonate
$\frac{1}{2}$ tablespoon (10ml) syrup	of soda
3 oz (95g) almonds, chopped	

Beat margarine, sugar and syrup until fluffy. Mix all ingredients together until thoroughly blended. Shape into a roll and chill. Cut into rings and place on baking sheet. Bake in a moderate oven until golden. They keep well in a tin.

Elizabeth Buchan, Piddletrenthide

Snacks, Savouries and
Sandwiches

Egg and Celery Casserole
(Serves 4)

1½ oz (45g) butter
3 tablespoons (60ml) milk
3–4 tablespoons (60-80ml)
   cooked peas (optional)
1 can condensed celery soup
4 oz (115g) grated cheese

4 hardboiled eggs
1 medium-sized onion (peeled
   and chopped)
1 tablespoon (20ml)
   breadcrumbs

Melt ¾oz (20g) butter, add onion and cook until soft but not coloured. Add soup, milk and most of the cheese. Stir over low heat for 3–4 minutes. Add peas (if used) and chopped eggs. Put in a buttered fireproof dish. Mix remaining cheese with breadcrumbs and sprinkle on top. Dot with butter and bake in moderate oven (375°F, Gas Mark 5, 190°C) for 15-20 minutes.

Joan Ralph, Piddletrenthide

Cheese Sables

3 oz (95g) grated cheese
1 beaten egg
3 oz (95g) plain flour

Salt and pepper
3 oz (95g) butter

Rub butter into flour until mixture resembles breadcrumbs. Add cheese and season to taste. Press mixture together to form a dough. Leave in refrigerator for a few minutes if mixture is too sticky to roll out. Roll into an oblong. Cut into strips about 2 inches (5cm) wide. Brush with beaten egg and cut strips into triangles. Place sables on a baking dish lined with greaseproof paper and bake for approximately 10 minutes in oven 375°F, Gas Mark 5 or 190°C until golden brown.

J. P. Andrew, Plush

Leek Supper Dish

Clean some leeks and boil in salted water until nearly cooked. Strain. Wrap each leek in a slice of cooked ham. Place them in a shallow dish and pour a thick cheese sauce over them. Sprinkle with a little grated cheese and some cayenne pepper and brown in a hot oven for about 20 minutes.

Muriel Pike, Piddletrenthide

Scrambled Eggs and Chicken Livers
(A supper dish for two)

Fry 2 or 3 chicken livers in butter, having first cut them in small pieces. Scramble 4 eggs and add a dessertspoon (10ml) of cream. Mix with the chicken livers. Fry triangles of bread in butter until golden brown, and place on top of liver and egg mixture.

Noel Slade, Plush

Raw Tattie Fry
(Serves 2–4)

6 slices of streaky bacon   4 large potatoes, thinly sliced
1 large onion $\frac{1}{2}$ pt (275ml) water
Salt and pepper

Fry bacon lightly and add thinly sliced onion. Fry for about 4 minutes, turning. Add potatoes and season to taste. Pour water over to within about $\frac{1}{4}$ inch ($\frac{1}{2}$cm) of top. Put on lid and simmer until 'tatties' are soft. After approximately $\frac{1}{2}$ hour leave top off to crisp up.

Jill Uht, Piddletrenthide

Celery and Bacon Casserole
(Serves 4)

2 heads of celery or a 20-oz (560g) can of celery hearts
½ pt (275ml) cheese sauce
4–6 rashers of lean bacon

2–3 tablespoons (40-60ml) breadcrumbs
1 tablespoon (20ml) grated cheese

Cut bacon into pieces and partially cook. Prepare celery, cut into pieces and boil. Make cheese sauce. Put bacon and celery into heatproof dish and pour cheese sauce over. Mix breadcrumbs with grated cheese and sprinkle on top. Bake in a moderate oven until browned on top.

Joan Ralph, Piddletrenthide

Savoury Creamed Eggs
(Serves 4)

In a liquidiser mix 4 hardboiled eggs, 1 large tin consommé and 5 oz (145g) of double cream. Flavour with anchovy essence. Pour into individual cocotte dishes and chill until set. Pour a little consommé over each dish and re-chill. Serve sprinkled with chopped parsley.

Amy Till, Piddletrenthide

Hawker's Quiche

Base

8 oz (225g) plain flour
4 oz (115g) fat

Pinch of salt

Rub ingredients together until they are like fine breadcrumbs.
Mix with water into pastry. Grease a flan tin and line it with the
pastry.

Filling

8 oz (225g) bacon (the cheaper
  cut the better)
1 small onion, chopped

3 eggs beaten with a little milk
3 oz (95g) grated cheese
Seasoning

Cut the bacon into small strips and fry gently with onion. Put
bacon and onion on the pastry base. Sprinkle with the cheese and
add the beaten eggs and the seasoning. Cook in a pre-heated
oven (375°F, Gas Mark 5, 190°C) until mixture is set and
golden brown.

Ann Hawker, Piddletrenthide

Shrimp and Cheese Ramekins

3 eggs
3 oz (95g) grated Cheddar
  cheese
½ pt (275ml) double cream
Juice of 1 fresh lemon

8 oz (225g) Weymouth Bay
  shrimps (peeled)
Salt
Black pepper
Paprika

Pre-heat oven to 400°F, Gas Mark 6 (200°C). Butter 8 ramekin
dishes. Divide the shrimps equally between the ramekins. Beat
the eggs, add cheese, double cream, seasoning and lemon juice
and pour over the shrimps. Stand dishes in large tin containing ½
inch of water and cook for about 20 minutes. Dust with paprika
and decorate with a sprig of parsley.

Sallie Firrell, Piddletrenthide

Pike's Piddle Pâté
(A cheap and easy pâté for beginners)

6 oz (170g) chicken livers
6 oz (170g) pig's liver
1 onion (chopped finely)
1 clove of garlic

½ pt (275ml) chicken stock
1 oz (30g) butter
2 tablespoons (40ml) sherry
1 teaspoon (2ml) lemon juice

Saute the onion in the butter. Slice the livers and add to the onions with the crushed garlic and the stock. Simmer until tender. Cool, transfer to an electric blender and blend until smooth. Add the sherry and lemon juice and stir well. Add seasoning. Line a cake tin with streaky bacon and put in the pâté. Put more bacon on the top. Cook in a moderate oven for an hour. Refrigerate until required.

Muriel Pike, Piddletrenthide

Dorset Country-Style Pâté

½ lb (225g) minced steak
½ lb (225g) sausage meat, chopped finely
½ lb (225g) lamb's liver, chopped finely
2 oz (155g) white breadcrumbs
1 onion, chopped finely

1 clove of garlic (optional)
1 tablespoon (20ml) chopped parsley
1 egg
¼ teaspoon (1ml) mixed herbs
2 bay leaves
A few whole peppercorns

Mix all ingredients together. Put into greased tin. Cover with foil and place in roasting tin half full of water. Bake at 350°F or Gas Mark 4 (180°C) for 2 hours. Pour off excess liquid and leave until cold.

John Firrell, Piddletrenthide

Smoked Salmon Pâté

2½ lb (225g) smoked salmon pieces
2 tablespoons (40ml) oil
2 oz (55g) butter
Pinch of cayenne pepper

1–2 tablespoons (20-40ml) lemon juice
2–4 tablespoons (40-80ml) double cream

Soften butter, add oil and mix well. Mince (or chop finely) smoked salmon and gradually stir into butter mixture and mix well. Add lemon juice, double cream and pepper.

Elizabeth Durham, Piddletrenthide

Five-Minute Fish Spread

Mash 2 hardboiled eggs with the contents of a tin of sardines (central bones removed) and a small carton of cottage cheese. Put in the refrigerator until required.

Sandwich Fillings

Cream cheese and chives

Egg, onion and mayonnaise

Contents of a tin of luncheon meat and half a small onion, liquidised

Chopped dates and walnuts moistened with a little honey

Minced ham moistened with a thick cheese sauce

Minced tongue with tomato ketchup

Minced chicken with mayonnaise, mustard and cress

Mock Crab

2 oz (55g) margarine
2 skinned tomatoes
1 well-beaten egg

2 oz (55g) grated cheese
1 small chopped onion

Put onion in top of double saucepan. Simmer and then add tomatoes, margarine, cheese and, lastly, egg. Allow to thicken *but not boil.* Can be served hot on toast or cold as a sandwich spread.

Peggy Cake, Plush

Savoury Supper
(Excellent for late guests. Serves 4)

4 oz (115g) cooked ham or
  grilled bacon
½ lb (225g) spaghetti
6 oz (170g) finely grated
  cheese

Small chopped onion
Can of condensed tomato soup
Mushrooms and tomatoes to
  garnish

Cook spaghetti in boiling salted water. Drain. Add rest of ingredients, cook over low heat for 10 minutes. Place in a well-buttered oven-proof dish and put tomatoes and some cheese on the top. Stand in a tin of cold water. Cook in a slow oven (300°F, Gas Mark 2 or 150°C) for approximately ¾ hour. (This will keep longer in the oven without becoming dry because of the tin of water.) Serve with french bread and celery.

Patricia Weeks, Piddletrenthide

Onion and Potato Cake

1 lb (455g) potatoes	Salt and pepper
2 large onions	Butter
8 oz (225g) shortcrust pastry	

Peel and quarter the potatoes and onions and boil until soft.
Make up 8 oz pastry and roll into a circle. Add the potatoes and
onions in chunks on to half the circle and season well. Add dabs
of butter on the top. Seal the edges well and fold over to form a
half circle. Flute the edges and add a milk wash. Bake in a
moderate oven for ½ hour. Serve hot or cold.

> Joan Chandler, The Brace of Pheasants, Plush

Stuffed Cauliflower

Boil a cauliflower, but don't let it fall to pieces. With a sharp
knife, cut out a hole from the heart of the cauliflower. Fill the
hole with well-seasoned minced meat. Some red pepper should
be added. Make a good white sauce, mix some grated cheese into
it and pour it over the cauliflower. Put the dish into the oven to
heat through. Serve very hot.

> A. H. Waterfield, White Lackington

Richelieu Eggs

Cut 4 fair-sized tomatoes in two and remove the seeds. Fry
lightly in 1 oz (30g) of butter. Cut some rounds of toast a little
larger than the tomatoes. Beat 3 eggs in a saucepan, add a large
spoonful of cream, ¾ oz (23g) butter and seasoning to taste. Add
some chopped pimento (peppers) if you wish. Stir over low heat
until the mixture is creamy and a bit firm. Put each tomato on to
a round of toast, fill with the mixture, garnish with parsley and
serve.

> A. H. Waterfield, White Lackington

Quichy Pizza

	Scone Dough
½ lb (225g) tomatoes	6 oz (170g) flour
1 onion	½ teaspoon (2ml) salt
1 clove garlic	½ teaspoon (2ml) dry mustard
1 oz (30g) butter	1½ oz (45g) butter
1 teaspoon (4ml) tomato purée	2 oz (55g) grated Cheddar
Pinch of mixed herbs	cheese
1 tablespoon (20ml) parsley	¼ pt (150ml) milk
1 teaspoon (4ml) mustard	
Salt and pepper	
3 oz (95g) grated Cheddar	
cheese	
6 anchovy fillets	
Olives	

Skin and chop tomatoes. Peel and chop onion. Crush garlic. Put butter in pan with onion and garlic. Cook. Add tomatoes, purée, herbs, parsley, mustard, cheese and seasoning. Cook.

Sieve flour, salt and mustard. Rub in butter. Add cheese and milk until it forms a dough. Roll and put in greased baking tin 11½ inches (20cm) by 7½ inches (10cm) or a round one.

Brush dough with anchovy oil and put mixture in it. Criss-cross with anchovies and dot with olives. Cook 425°F, Gas Mark 7 (220°C) for about 25 minutes.

Jillie Edwards, Piddletrenthide

FROM THE PAST

The author of *Domestic Cookery* observed that a very good meal may be bestowed on poor people in a thing called 'Brewis', which is thus made:
'Cut a very thick upper crust of bread and put it into the pot where salt beef is boiling, and nearly ready. It will attach some of the fat and when swelled out will be no unpalatable dish to those who rarely taste meat.' (Extracted from *The Cook* by W. G. Lewis published by Houlston and Stoneman, London 1846.)

J. E. Morris, Piddletrenthide

Pickles, Preserves and Sauces

Apple and Tomato Chutney

6 large tomatoes
1½ pt (90ml) vinegar
3 teaspoons (12ml) salt
4 small onions
6 apples

1 green pepper
3 cups (540g) brown sugar
Mixed spice
1 cup (180g) stoned raisins

Chop the tomatoes, apples, raisins and pepper finely, add remainder of ingredients, tying in muslin bag. Boil 1½ hours. Remove the spice bag, turn the pickle into sterilised jars and seal.

Runner Bean Chutney

2 lb (900g) runner beans
   (chopped)
1¼ pt (725ml) vinegar
A few raisins
1 teaspoon (4ml) mustard

1½ tablespoons (30ml)
   cornflour
1½ lb (680g) onions
2 lb (900g) demerara sugar
1 oz (30g) turmeric (herb)

Cook beans and onions in ¼ pint (150ml) vinegar for 15 minutes. Add rest of the ingredients. Boil 10 minutes and pot. A delicious sweet chutney.

Mrs V. Ralph, Alton Pancras

Marrow Pickle

1 lb (455g) marrow
½ lb (225g) sugar
4 cloves
1½ oz (45g) dry mustard

1½ oz (45g) ground ginger
2 pt (1.15l) vinegar
6 chillies
½ oz (15g) turmeric (herb)

Cut the marrow into square pieces, put into a bowl and sprinkle with salt. Leave overnight and strain next morning. Boil other ingredients together for 10 minutes, stirring all the time. Add the marrow cubes and boil until tender. Put into warm jars and cover when cold.

Mrs D. Coulthard, Piddletrenthide

Gooseberry Marmalade

2 lb (900g) gooseberries
Juice and grated rind of one
  lemon

2 pt (1.15l) water
3 lb (1.35K) granulated sugar

Top and tail the gooseberries and place in a preserving pan with
the rest of the ingredients. Bring to the boil and continue boiling
for $1\frac{1}{4}$ hours or until set. Test for setting by placing a very small
quantity on a saucer and cooling. If a skin forms on top the
preserve is cooked. Put into warm jars and cover when cold.

Mrs D. Coulthard, Piddletrenthide

Three Fruit Marmalade

6 Seville oranges
3 sweet oranges

2 lemons

Slice fruit thinly. Take out seeds. Weigh fruit and add 3 pints
(180ml) water to each pound of fruit. Use some of the water to
cover the seeds. Allow to stand for 24 hours. Boil pulp for two
hours – seeds for about 1 hour. Then drain liquor from seeds
into fruit. Allow to stand for 24 hours after boiling. Then add 1
lb (455g) sugar to each pound of pulp and stir in. Boil until clear
and set.

Miss W. Murrell, Plush

Four Fruit Marmalade

2 apples	2 lemons
1 grapefruit	Water
2 sweet oranges	Sugar

Peel and core the apples, and put them through a mincing machine. Cut the other fruit in halves and squeeze out the juice. Throw away the pips. Put the squeezed skins through the mincer, then add them to the minced apples, together with the juice. Measure the whole, add three times the quantity of water, and leave to soak for 24 hours. Simmer for 1½ hours, then measure the pulp, and to every pint of pulp add 1 pound of sugar. Boil for 40 minutes, or until it will set when tested.

Mrs Chanter, Alton Pancras

Japonica Jelly

Pick as many fruits as you can from an ordinary ornamental japonica bush, wash them and cut them up into small pieces. Put them in a saucepan or preserving pan and cover with water. Stew until pulpy. Put the pulp in a jelly bag and drip overnight. In the morning, put the dripped juice in a pan with sugar (one lb (455g) of sugar to one pint (575ml) of juice). Add the juice of one lemon. Cook on a low heat until sugar has melted, then boil fast until the jelly starts to wrinkle and set when a spoonful is put on a cold saucer. Pour into jars and tie down in the usual way. This makes a fragrant and delicately flavoured jelly.

Muriel Pike, Piddletrenthide

Fig and Lemon Preserve

2 lb (900g) figs with stalks removed	4 lemons
2 pt (1.15l) water	3 lb (1.35K) sugar

Wash the figs, cut them into small pieces and soak in the water
for 24 hours. Turn into a preserving pan, add the sugar and
simmer until the sugar has melted. Skim. Add grated rind and
juice of the lemons and boil fairly fast until the figs have turned
into pulp and the jam sets when tested on a cool saucer. Pour
into jars and tie down.

Muriel Pike, Piddletrenthide

Mother-in-Law's Mincemeat

1 lb (455g) beef suet
1 lb (455g) caster sugar
1 lb (455g) currants
1 lb (455g) raisins
½ lb (225g) mixed peel

½ lb (225g) chopped or minced
apple
1 teaspoon (4ml) nutmeg
Juice of 2 lemons
Wineglass of brandy

Mix all the ingredients. Leave 24 hours. Mix again. Pack in jars.

Pat Green, Piddletrenthide

Red Tomato Relish

3 lb (1.35K) tomatoes
4 large onions
1½ tablespoons (30ml) dry
mustard
1 tablespoon (20ml) curry
powder

1 lb (455g) sugar
1 tablespoon (20ml) salt
5 chillies
Vinegar
1 tablespoon (20ml) cornflour

Cut up tomatoes and sprinkle with salt. Slice the onions and put
with the tomatoes to stand all night. Drain off the water. Put
into a saucepan, just cover with vinegar and boil hard for 5
minutes. Mix mustard and curry powder with a little water and
add this together with the chillies and sugar. Boil ¾ hour until
mixed to a paste. Add the cornflour to thicken and boil for a
further 5 minutes.

Audrey Condon, Piddletrenthide

Barbecue Sauce

2 oz (155g) butter
1 large onion, chopped
1 level teaspoon (4ml) tomato
   paste
2 tablespoons (40ml) vinegar
¼ pt (150ml) water

2 tablespoons (40ml) demerara
   sugar
2 level teaspoons (8ml) dry
   mustard
2 tablespoons (40ml)
   Worcestershire sauce

Melt butter and fry onion until soft. Stir in the tomato paste and cook for a further 3 minutes. Blend remaining ingredients to a smooth cream and add to the onion mixture. Simmer for about 10 minutes. If liked, add a little cornflour to make it thicker. This freezes well in small quantities.

Mint Sauce
(Keeps for one year or more)

1 teacupful (180g) of finely
   chopped mint

½ pt (275ml) vinegar
6 oz (170g) sugar

Boil vinegar and sugar together. Remove from heat. Add chopped mint. Bottle when cold. When required for use, add more vinegar.

Joan Ralph, Piddletrenthide

Rhubarb Jam with Elderflower

6 lb (2.75K) rhubarb, washed
   and cut
6 lb (2.75K) sugar

1 breakfastcup (275ml) of
   elderflowers, tied in a
   muslin bag

Stand the rhubarb overnight in the sugar (no water). Next day boil for 15 minutes. Add elderflowers and continue to boil for a further 15 to 20 minutes. Remove elderflowers and pot up jam. Note: The elderflowers should be collected when they will shake from the stem.

Amy Till, Piddletrenthide

Marrow and Pineapple Jam
(Great-Great-Aunt Alicia's recipe from Tiverton)

Cut the marrow into pieces about one inch in thickness and to every 3 lb (1.35K) of marrow allow one small tin of pineapple pieces. Put in a bowl together with the pineapple juice and the grated rind of one large lemon. Add 3 lb (1.35K) of sugar and allow to stand until the next day. Then boil all together for $2\frac{1}{2}$ to 3 hours. Add the lemon juice just before it is ready to take up.

Muriel Pike, Piddletrenthide

Bullace Cheese

Bullaces

Sugar, $\frac{3}{4}$ lb (338g) to every 1lb (455g) pulp

Cook the fruit to a pulp, press through sieve and weigh. Add sugar. Put back into preserving pan, stir to dissolve sugar, and bring to the boil. Boil, stirring constantly as the mixture burns easily, until a little will set when tested. Pour into small jars and seal when cold.

Jill Uht, Piddletrenthide

Marrow Cream Cheese

2 lb (900g) marrow
$\frac{1}{4}$ lb (115g) butter

2 lb (900g) sugar
Rind and juice of 3 lemons

Peel marrow and take out seeds. Boil or steam until tender. Strain away all liquid and pass marrow through a sieve. Beat and put in a preserving pan with grated lemon rind and juice. Boil until it thickens, stirring all the time. Add butter and mix well together. Put in small jars and cover while hot. This will keep for months.

Grandma Young's Mayonnaise

3 eggs
2 breakfastcupfuls (550ml)
  milk
2 tablespoons (40ml) dried
  mustard
½ tablespoon (10ml) salt

4 tablespoons (80ml) vegetable
  oil
1 breakfastcupful (275ml)
  vinegar
4 tablespoons (80ml) caster
  sugar

Put oil, salt, mustard and sugar in a saucepan. Stir until smooth. Add eggs, well beaten, then vinegar, and lastly milk, adding gradually. Stir over a gentle heat until it thickens like custard. DO NOT BOIL. Bottle and cork when cold. This will keep a long time – but not in our house!

Patricia Weeks, Piddletrenthide

Drinks

Drinks

Citrus Whip
(Makes 1½ to 2 pints, 850ml – 1.15l)

2 medium oranges
¾ pt (425ml) water
1 medium lemon

3 tablespoons (60ml) caster
sugar

Slice fruit roughly and put some into liquidiser with some of the
water. Run for 5 seconds. Strain into jug. Repeat and when all
liquidised add sugar. Serve iced.

Audrey Condon, Piddletrenthide

Lemonade

4 lemons
2 pts (1.15l) water

2 lb (900g) sugar
1 oz (30g) citric acid

Grate rinds and squeeze juice from fruit. Add sugar and citric
acid. Cover with 2 pints (1.15l) boiling water. Leave 24 hours,
strain and bottle. Keeps for weeks.

Kathy Jakeman. Piddletrenthide

Plush Punch

2 bottle Spanish sauterne
1 bottle cider

¼ bottle brandy

Mix all ingredients together. This is very good for a party.

Peggy Cake, Plush

Friary 'Champagne'

1½ lb (850ml) sugar
2 tablespoons (40ml) white
   wine vinegar or white
   distilled vinegar

10 large heads of elderflower
1 gal. (5l) cold water
2 lemons

Place the sugar and the vinegar into a very large bowl. To this
you add the 10 large elderflower heads followed by the gallon of
cold water. Squeeze and quarter the lemons and add to the
mixture. Let it stand for 24 hours, stirring occasionally. After 24
hours, strain the mixture before bottling in screw-top bottles. It
is ready to drink after a few days, but beware: it is really fizzy!

Cider Punch
(Serves 10)

Combine 2 quarts (2½l) of cider with ½ bottle gin or vodka and ¼
bottle sherry. Wash and slice 2 unpeeled oranges and 1 lemon
and add these to the cider mixture with 3 tablespoons (60ml)
sugar. Crush 3 sprigs of fresh mint and add. Chill well. Just
before serving add 1 cold syphon of soda water or more if too
strong. Serve with ice or well chilled.

Jill Uht, Piddletrenthide

Home-Made Ginger Beer

Boil together for one hour 1 gal. (5l) water, 1 oz (30g) bruised
ginger and 1 lb (455g) sugar. Skim the liquor and pour into a
vessel containing ½ sliced lemon and ¼ oz (7g) cream of tartar.
Cool and add ½ teacupful (150ml) of yeast. Set it to work for
two days. Strain and bottle, stoppering or corking firmly. It will
be ready for use in a few days.

J. Morris, Piddletrenthide

Drinks

FROM THE PAST

Ancient recipes from a cookery book of the 1700s

Almond Shrub

Take 3 gallons of rum or brandy, 3 quarts of orange juice, the peel of three lemons, 3 lbs of loaf sugar, then 4 oz of bitter almonds, blanch and beat them fine, mix them all well together. Let it stand an hour to curdle, run it through a flannel bag several times till it is clear, then bottle for use.

Smyrna Raisin Wine

To 100 of raisins put 20 gallons of water, let it stand 14 days, then put it into your cask; when it has been in 6 months add to it 1 gallon of French brandy, and when it is fine bottle it.

Allan Ralph, Piddletrenthide

Oven Temperatures

Type of food	Centre oven temp °F	Thermostat setting	Heat of oven
Fruit Bottling	240°	$\frac{1}{4}$	
Stews	260°		Very cool
		$\frac{1}{2}$	
Custard and Egg Dishes Milk Puddings	280°		
		1	
	300°		Cool
Rich Fruit Cake		2	
	320°		
Slow Roasting Shortbread		3	Warm
	340°		
Plain Fruit Cake, Madeira Cake, Biscuits		4	Moderate
	360°		
Queen Cakes, Sponges	380°	5	
			Fairly hot
Plain Buns, Plate Tarts, Short Pastry	400°	6	
	420°		Hot
Scones Roasting		7	
	440°		
		8	
Puff and Flaky Pastry			
	460°		Very hot
		9	
	480°		

Vicarage Cold Pot

Take one vicar (not too stale)
Mix with one wife, marinaded in paint and wallpaper
Season with two sons, to add spice and variety
Stir together and place in one large, draughty vicarage with a
sprinkling of mice (the church variety) and a teaspoonful of
friendly ghosts
Cook for any length of time and enjoy the result throughout the
year

In order to forestall a riot,
And keep the whole family quiet,
I have said I will cook
All the things in this book . . .
And then we'll all go on a diet.

Heather Parry, Piddletrenthide Vicarage

Index